DON'T GET

SACKED

•IN•

RETIREMENT

A Financial Quarterback's
Playbook for Winning the Game

BRYON K. SPICER

Advantage

Published by Advantage, Charleston, South Carolina.
Member of Advantage Media Group.

ADVANTAGE is a registered trademark and the Advantage colophon is a trademark of Advantage Media Group, Inc.

Printed in the United States of America.

ISBN: 978-159932-304-6
LCCN: 2012939443

This publication is designed to provide accurate and authoritative information in regard to the subject matter covered. It is sold with the understanding that the publisher is not engaged in rendering legal, accounting, or other professional services. If legal advice or other expert assistance is required, the services of a competent professional person should be sought.

 Advantage Media Group is proud to be a part of the Tree Neutral® program. Tree Neutral offsets the number of trees consumed in the production and printing of this book by taking proactive steps such as planting trees in direct proportion to the number of trees used to print books. To learn more about Tree Neutral, please visit www.treeneutral.com. To learn more about Advantage's commitment to being a responsible steward of the environment, please visit www.advantagefamily.com/green

Advantage Media Group is a leading publisher of business, motivation, and self-help authors. Do you have a manuscript or book idea that you would like to have considered for publication? Please visit www.advantagefamily.com or call 1.866.775.1696

TABLE OF CONTENTS

ABOUT THE AUTHOR

Bryon K. Spicer, founder of Seniors Financial Services and Spicer Wealth Management, has devoted over three decades of his life to educating and assisting retirees and pre-retirees on how to plan for and protect their "Financial Security for their Golden Years."

An advocate for comprehensive financial and retirement planning, Spicer's goal is to help ensure that all components of a client's financial affairs work in collaboration. In short, he helps clients reach their retirement dreams.

Spicer has held several designations, including Certified Insurance Counselor. He co-authored the book "Issues of Aging" and published a book on charitable giving.

As an accounting major at Wright State University, Spicer became involved in the insurance business, eventually owning and operating small and large independent insurance agencies. That led to financial management: "Clients would tell me: 'Bryon, you're doing everything else, why not handle my investments?'"

Spicer began to specialize in retirement planning after his mother became seriously ill. "That got me thinking about issues older people face," he says. "I sold my insurance practices and down sized many of the other businesses I had an ownership in."

"Through continuing education and working with many national experts, I've acquired a breadth of knowledge. I strongly believe that you can always learn – and the more you learn, the more you learn what you don't know."

"That's why I spend hundreds of hours a year in continuing education. Taxes change, legal issues change, the products change. Congress is constantly changing. In short, I am continuously accumulating knowledge from experts in different areas."

He actively shares what he has learned. A sought-after speaker, Spicer regularly conducts workshops on many advanced financial topics for the public and special interest groups, and he has lectured at Ohio State University. Spicer is an approved member of the National Ethics Bureau, indicating the highest regard for integrity and ethical decision-making.

He provides counsel in all areas of finances, working to protect retirees' assets and create income plans to preserve their lifestyle. He assists in finding tools and strategies so retirees pay only their fair share of taxes and get a greater return on investments with lower market risk. He then focuses on helping retirees transfer their assets to their loved ones in the most efficient way possible while reducing costs of probate and estate taxes.

Spicer has been married to his wife, Kay, since 1985 and has one son. He and his family are active in their church, school, and sports associations, with Spicer holding several board positions in each.

INTO THE END ZONE

"There are those who are winners and know they are winners," the legendary football coach Bear Bryant once said. "Then there are the losers who know they are losers. Then there are those who are not winners, but don't know it. They're the ones for me. They never quit trying. They're the soul of our game."

It's all in the effort, in other words. It's about striving and dreaming, and diligently making the most of what you have. If you do that, you are bound to find out that you are a winner after all.

The role of a wealth adviser is much like a coach. It involves helping clients develop strategies and pursue their goals so they can be winners at season's end. But even more, it's like being a quarterback, right out there on the field with the teammates and facing the challenges together.

When a quarterback heads out to the field, he's working by the playbook that the team has developed, detailing all the strategies that may be needed in the game. He has done his homework and analyzed which play works best in each situation. He knows how to adjust those plays based on what's happening on the field. His experience and determination help lead his team to the win.

The quarterback does not "hope" that his play will work. He doesn't merely hope that the ball will fly true or the opposition will fumble. Nor does a wealth adviser just hope that the markets will edge ever upward and that his or her suggestions affecting your future will somehow work out.

These are not matters for wishful thinking. These are matters for carefully designed strategies, tried and proven, and implemented skillfully and wisely. You are significantly raising your chances of success by developing a powerful offense and defense.

It has been said both ways: The best defense is a good offense, and the best offense is a good defense. It's true in football, and it's true in life. In retirement, the latter strategy takes precedence, as we will see, yet you still will make all your best offensive plays appropriate for this stage of the game.

The goal of the game, of course, is to get into the end zone victoriously.

I recently attended a client's funeral. "This is my wealth adviser," his widow said when introducing me, "but more importantly, this is my friend." And I thought back to the day that couple first came to my office, with all those cares and concerns, and how we began to focus together on things that mattered, on quality-of-life issues. Spending more time with the grandkids and spending more time with the causes that they believed in – that's what it was all about, really. It was about helping them reach their dreams in retirement and taking those worries away.

A typical client, very often a husband and wife, comes to us with a variety of concerns. They may feel that what they are doing is not working. They're unsure whether they are paying too much in taxes; they are not sure they'll have enough money to last throughout their retirement; and they don't know how much they might lose in estate taxes and probate fees. And if they should have a health-care crisis, they just don't know whether they could make it.

We start with some planning that helps them focus on goals: how to be sure they can maintain their accustomed lifestyle for the rest of their life and not run out of money. How to guard against paying too much in taxes. How to leave whatever's left over to their loved ones, or to the charities and causes they care about. We look to do so as efficiently as possible so that those people and those causes – not the government – get the money. If this were a football game, you could say we were guiding them into the end zone.

Your Coach and Your Quarterback

What it's really all about is peace of mind, and a wealth adviser can't just lay out a lot of figures and statistics and expect to connect with people. A good adviser must listen to their stories – and that includes opening up the closet to see all the good stuff and all the bad stuff. There are times when the Kleenexes come out because we broach matters that are very touchy. It's difficult, for example, for a couple to talk about a child who passed away before them. That violates the circle of life, and though such matters inevitably come up during the course of financial advising, it's never without pain. It feels to the couple as if it happened yesterday.

What happens in life affects one's ability to make wise decisions. A football coach knows this. Each player has his great days and his bad ones. And a financial coach must know this too. Clients often call not because they want specific financial advice but because they look to the adviser the way a football player would look to the coach. "Here's somebody who will truly give me an unbiased opinion," they think, "without judging."

People will come in with myths and misconceptions on which they are basing decisions, and therefore not performing up to par. They become very frustrated. Just as a coach helps a player improve his performance, a retirement quarterback can lay out the facts about how the marketplace really works and the tools that are available to use it to their best advantage. He or she motivates, counsels, guides – that is, does a lot of coaching to help the client get through the frustrations.

The retirement quarterback not only helps to organize the game plan, but also helps with the spot decisions when the ball is in play: "Here are the investment tools that may help you get to your goal safely and securely. Here's how they will affect your tax return. Here's how they affect your distribution plan." You have to consider how each decision fits into your overall game plan and then make the calls and take the steps to advance safely and securely toward the goals. The adviser helps the client set up an effective defense, so that when those heavy players start pressing down – market risk issues, taxes and fees, Medicare and catastrophic illnesses, probate, so many others – a plan is in place to deal with them.

As you head into retirement, you're pushing hard toward that goal line. You are striving to get safely and securely through those retirement years. At the season's end, you'll rest well knowing you played your best and won the respect of the crowds. No more worries: You'll have the lifestyle you have grown accustomed to. You won't run out of money. You won't fumble the ball just to see it swept away by the tax man, or some attorney. Instead, all your hard work will be your legacy. Your loved ones, and your cherished causes, will remember and appreciate you for what you accomplished. You put in a good game.

You Need a Playbook

And yet, even in the final moments of a game that seemed yours to win, when victory seemed assured, bad things can happen. The scoreboard can flash some cruel numbers. You have seen it happen too often to others. And it could happen to you: Unless you have an effective plan in place, you can get tackled just short of the goal line. Instead of leaving money to your children or charities, you risk giving it away instead to market losses; to the federal or state governments, with their probate and estate levies; or to lawyers who want a generous share as well.

You can't expect to win the game, in other words, unless you have a playbook. You'll make it to some end zone, one way or another, but when the big buzzer sounds, it's unlikely you'll have scored many field goals and touchdowns along the way.

Look back at 2008 for examples of retirees without the proper playbook. Some lost half their nest egg in the market correction. Let's say a couple had a million dollars and were taking out five percent a year, or $50,000, thinking they couldn't possibly ever run out of money – and all of a sudden they have half a million and were drawing away ten percent a year just to keep their lifestyle the same. "Forever" didn't seem quite so certain.

That's no way to live, even if you can make it through life. You can't move forward confidently if you don't know what to expect. You need a plan. You need clarity about your goals so that you can sleep well at night. You won't lie in bed staring at the ceiling wondering what's going to happen the next day if you know that you can make it through no matter what the opposition brings your way.

It reminds me of that Bear Bryant quote. People who are so sure they are good are often the ones who are lacking in efficiency. People who are less sure, on the other hand, are likely to seek out help and find greater success that way. They're humble enough to say, "Hey, I can't do this on my own."

They seek out an expert, the way you do when you need a doctor. If you have the flu, the family doctor is fine. If you have a brain tumor, you'll want a neurosurgeon. You must seek out the expertise that truly will help your condition. If you think you can be your own expert, whether in medicine or finances, you're playing with life issues. No matter your skill and guts and stamina, you need to be amenable to good coaching, to go by the playbook and commit to it. It will guide you through goals both short term and long term, whether you're looking to go one or two yards or accomplish a twenty-yard pass – or whether you're looking for money to pay the daily bills or to grow your portfolio for the years ahead.

The earlier you develop that playbook, the better. Even if you have waited until retirement, the sooner you get one, the more successful you're going to be – even if you're twenty years into retirement. You can always improve the game. You can always do better with some guidance and counsel. The sooner you get it, the more likely you will be able to recover from earlier mistakes and get the best performance with the least amount of effort.

The playbook, of course, isn't developed at the start of each game. It's done well in advance, so that the players can anticipate what might be coming at them and how they'll react in a given situation. You want to anticipate what those defensive players may do. How are you managing your finances? What kind of financial tools are you using to preserve and grow your wealth? Are you positioning your finances to pay the least amount of tax? The tax man is a brawny player trying hard to set you back.

It's important to design strategies for every one of those players – Medicare, catastrophic illness, market risk, probate, taxes, fees, debts. How will you deal with them? What's the most efficient way to get around them? If you have anticipated them in your financial playbook, you are ready to respond when the game brings them your way. Like a quarterback, you and your wealth adviser will make those calls, implementing different strategies as conditions on the field warrant.

The coach doesn't just hand out copies of a playbook and suggest the team members check it out when they can. They sit down and review it, study it, strategize. That way they know the fundamentals when it comes time to modify it – as surely will happen, since nothing works perfectly either in life or in football. Even the rules sometimes change.

Adjusting When the Game Has Changed

A football team that uses the same strategies no matter what's going on in the game will be doomed to fail. Once, you might have loved to strive for those twenty- or forty-yard passes in your investments. Now you want to go for three, six, ten yards at a time, always wary of interceptions.

Generally, when you're at the end of the game and you're winning, you won't be as likely to go for the big plays. More and more retirees will move away from the market risk side, meaning they won't routinely go for those long passes. They're more comfortable using safer plays that will just get them one, three, four yards at a time.

In retirement, preservation of money becomes so much more critical than getting that extra one or two percent increase in growth – particularly when you already have that big lead. That's not to say you're giving up on growth. But your focus is that you're comfortable with a five or six percent return versus trying to get an eight or a ten percent return and taking more market risk and possibly losing.

Yet when it comes to financial tools, a lot of people keep taking the same approach and expecting the results to get better. That, as they say, is the definition of insanity. For example, the financial tools that worked for our grandparents were real estate and putting money in the bank. Those tools don't work as well anymore.

Remember the old wringer washer? Remember the old push mower with the rotary blades? They still work, though not as well as we might like. We've changed the tools we use around our home to move to safer, more efficient ones. We need to do the same thing with our finances. Your financial tools need to adapt and change over time to ones that are more efficient and safer to use. Don't keep using a tool just because you're used to it. With time, far better methods evolve.

When you retire, you find yourself responsible for maintaining your own income. You no longer have that paycheck coming in, so you have to create that paycheck. That means you have to change the way you manage money. You can't focus on growth. You have to focus on preservation, and that takes a set of skills different from what you likely grew accustomed to in your investment life. It's hard to change that mindset. You don't necessarily know how. And wisdom is knowing when it's time to bring in someone else to advise you.

The additional people who will be working with you and reviewing your financial playbook include your CPA, your attorney, your insurance agent, your stockbroker. If the retirement quarterback is doing his job properly, he's coordinating all of these other team professionals to make sure you are reaching your goals as safely and securely as possible, and that it's always your interests that are being served, not the other professionals.

Everybody on the team has a different job to do. A CPA will figure your taxes but not help you minimize them. An attorney will write up your documents but may not mention that a trust would be a good option. The professionals do their duties, but you also need someone to coordinate and help you consider the various financial tools to bring you the most efficient results possible.

Your professional teammates are your offense. They are your players on the line, protecting you. They'll help you develop strategies to deal with issues as they arise. Your tax adviser, for example, might help you with an offensive strategy with your retirement account, moving it from a taxable bucket of money into one that is less subject to taxation and keeps you from getting beaten up year after year. Your offensive line can get those opponents out of the game for you.

In estate planning, for example, you need to deal with tax issues, minimize or eliminate probate expenses, and decide whether the money is distributed in a lump sum or over time. You may have questions about how you can protect that inheritance from creditors or divorce proceedings. You may wonder how best to leave money to an heir whom you consider irresponsible or immature: To leave him or her a lump sum would be like giving a drink to an alcoholic.

The type of strategies that you employ, offensive or defensive, also will change during your investment career, just as it changes during the course of a football game. When you're talking about money invested in the market, every financial tool will fall into one of three categories.

You will have safe tools with guarantees of principal and a very low, modest rate of return. They will give you liquidity but not a lot of asset growth. There are times when you need those one or two yards. In addition, you may have investments that take on more market risk. That's when you're playing for the long pass, going for growth potential. You can still have liquidity, but you accept less safety, more risk for more gain.

In between the safer and the riskier financial tools is a category called hybrid or linked tools. Those take advantage of market potential yet retain safety – you participate, to an extent, in market gains but never in market losses. If equities zoom up thirty percent, you might realize, say, twenty percent. If they plummet, as in 2008, you get a zero return. Many retirees would be better off today if they had avoided this market loss and received a zero return.

An effective strategy requires a balanced employment of those safe, growth and hybrid tools from your playbook. You should be constantly adjusting your plays to make sure your approach works in any given situation.

It's crucial, in any case, to keep your portfolio diversified. Not doing so is like having only one play in your playbook. Let's say I retired from Procter & Gamble and most of my retirement money is in Procter & Gamble stock. I'm going to live and die with what I get out of that one stock. A better approach is to diversify and have some of my money in the safe tools, some money in hybrid, and some money in Procter & Gamble stock and maybe a few other stocks, and by doing that, I'm going to have a more consistent result. I'm going to be able to get down the field a lot more safely.

Knowing which strategy to employ at any given time depends on what's happening in the economy – on what you learn from your advisers, and what you hear about trends. If you know what you're facing – the tax rules, the probate rules, your exposure to catastrophic illness, etc. – then you can develop a good offensive strategy that anticipates those issues and minimizes them when they arise. How will those elements influence your lifestyle or your spouse's lifestyle if you are gone?

If all of a sudden, for example, you start spending $8,000 or $10,000 a month in a nursing facility, what effect will that have on your assets and on your loved ones? Will they be able to maintain their lifestyle? Those are considerations that need to be in the playbook. The players coming at us tend to be the same ones they have always been, yet sometimes they seem to pack a bigger wallop than ever. We must be ready.

Scoring Six, Three, and Extra Points

As you know, in football you can score six, you can score three, or you can go for extra points. As you prepare for a fruitful retirement, you can also think of your finances that way.

As you head down the field to your retirement, it makes sense to focus on scoring those sixes. You have to get into the end zone and make those touchdowns. You need to build a foundation for your hopes and dreams, developing a secure retirement income that safeguards your quality of life. That income cannot be subject to market factors – you need to know, regardless of what happens in the economy, that you won't run out of money and have to endure a lower standard of living.

Along the way, you'll be going for the field goals. That's when you score three. Scoring three would be enhancing your income by anticipating taxes and positioning your finances to pay the least amount possible. There are two ways to create wealth – you can either get better returns with lower risk, or you can reduce fees and expenses. Taxes are an expense that most people need to address more critically. For example, as we will see, you may have investments that are throwing off what is known as phantom income tax. You actually owe tax on money that you may not have received or that you're not using for living expenses. And that doesn't make a lot of sense. Why pay tax on money you're not using? Your strategy should be to pay only your fair share of taxes; otherwise, you'll be constantly hooking to the right or left and missing the goal posts.

On the football field, the players go for the extra points – striving to get the ball through the uprights one more time. From a retirement planning standpoint, extra points means making sure that whatever's left over goes efficiently to your heirs and to the causes that are dear to you. If you can avoid the costs of probate and keep your money away from the attorneys and tax man so that more of it goes into the hands of your loved ones and favorite causes, you're getting those extra points.

It can't happen without good planning. There won't be an opportunity for extra points unless you have those touchdowns first. And you won't get those extra points if you haven't properly set up your will or trust. The money won't go to your loved ones and charities in the manner and amount that you had hoped.

Getting the touchdown and the field goals and extra points are all crucial elements of winning the game. Your plan has to include every strategy, not just one. A wise coach or a wise retirement quarterback knows that everything contributes toward winning the game. There are times, for example, when tax strategies will give you a consistent return, even when the touchdowns aren't coming. You can win the game by reliably kicking those field goals. And the extra points can make all the difference. You can get comfortably through life and through retirement, but if you didn't score those extra points, the final score won't be high enough for you to really make it into the hall of fame.

When you're trying to go for the extra points, retirement accounts may be one of the worst accounts to have because they are not only subject to income tax but they may also be subject to estate tax. You may think you have scored a touchdown with half a million dollars in a retirement account, but was that truly a successful play? In truth, you're passing tax liability down to your kids. More than half your money may be taken away in the end zone. No extra points. But before you get into that situation, as we will see, you can do some end runs that can bring victory for you and your heirs. Good planning makes all the difference, not just in your own lifetime but far, far beyond, into the lifetimes of your children and your grandchildren.

Winning strategies are similar in many aspects of life. There are themes in our life that are universal, and I think it applies to both winning financially and winning on a sports field, no matter what the game is.

Years ago, a client came to me concerned that he might be paying too much in taxes on his investments. His stockbroker was pounding his chest, pointing to a twelve percent return for several years. But a look at my client's tax return showed a $10,000 tax liability tied to that investment – meaning his net return was four percent. In three years, we had eliminated that tax and raised the net return to eight percent.

This was an investor who was scoring some sixes but wasn't paying much attention to the threes. If you're doing the same, your gross return might be impressive, but you could be making someone very, very happy whom you don't particularly care about. The tax man would happily keep accepting your contribution to the treasury. Your broker would happily keep trumpeting your gross return. Let them go find their own ways to make themselves happy, but not at your expense.

And that includes the Internal Revenue Service. This has been established innumerable times: There's nothing illegal or immoral about positioning your finances to pay the least amount of tax. You need pay only what is required by the tax code. If you follow one set of rules and guidelines, you pay this much. If you follow another set of rules and guidelines, you get to pay less. The IRS doesn't care as long as you follow the rules.

Most people are uninformed about how to use the tax code to their advantage. That's where tax planning becomes a valuable tool. "Man, this looks too good to be true," clients occasionally tell me when I point out a beneficial tax strategy that is perfectly permissible under the tax code. But the rules are there, and if you follow them, you reap the benefit. It can be significant, especially when reducing the capital gains or ordinary income tax on certain accounts. You can get a lot more efficiency when balancing your positions between safe and hybrid tools and market risk. A professional in tax planning can help you find those breaks. Your teammates have your back.

This is certain: If you do not have a strategy, you will pay more in taxes. That's the default position. You should do what you are allowed to do. If you don't know about those strategies, that's understandable. They can be complex, and they change.

That's why you trust your retirement quarterback. It's a recurring theme: The more you learn, the more you learn you don't know, as in so many things in life. And that's what helps to nurture a spirit both humble and determined – and makes you the "soul of the game," the kind of player who would make Coach Bryant proud.

CHAPTER 1

DRIVING FOR THE GOAL LINE

Retirement Dreams and Pitfalls

As an exultant football team closes in on victory at the end of a big game, the players feel the jubilation of accomplishment: They are reaching their goal – a winning score, perhaps a championship. Their skills and innate drive have served them well, but something else has compelled them: a sense of direction. They could never have gotten this far, in the game or in the season, without a good game plan and good coaching. A successful team must be fundamentally physically fit, with the stamina to adapt to changing circumstances.

And so it goes, too, for one's retirement years. If your years of planning and gathering have left you financially fit, and you have developed a retirement strategy that can adapt both to changing economies and changes in your life, then you can enter the end zone with that sense of elation and the knowledge that success is yours.

In retirement, you want to focus on what is important to you and live a bountiful life – not worry whether you'll run out of money before you die. The pressure, most certainly, is on. After you get that final paycheck and your salary ends, you need to create your own paycheck and maintain your lifestyle. That feeling of great responsibility can be unsettling. All you have done in life, all of the money you have made, all your advances in the game are on the line as you head toward that final goal.

It's human nature to feel that pressure, but it's also an exciting time. You've worked hard and sacrificed to get to this point, and now you can do the things you have wanted to do – travel, spend time with the grandchildren, volunteer for charitable work. Your years ahead can be fun and meaningful.

And yet, it's also human to lie awake worrying about whether you'll make the right plays, whether something might go wrong. Will you have enough money or run out during retirement? If you become severely ill, how will that affect your spouse and family – not to mention you – emotionally and financially? A million questions may be swirling in your head.

For Better or Worse, You're Not Alone

Rest assured: You are not alone. I know how it feels because I've worked closely with so many souls facing those same questions – thousands of people over the years. And it's easy to dispel some of those concerns. Just as a new football player can find the prospect of a tackle daunting, so too can it trouble a retiree to anticipate a financial hit – and yet it's that very anticipation that builds the skills to face and overcome the challenge.

It comes down to this: You can have peace of mind knowing you'll have enough money throughout your retirement to maintain your lifestyle. That's really the biggest concern – the fear of not having accumulated enough to hedge for inflation or to deal with a catastrophic illness. And that sense of anxiety is a major motivator to start taking a closer look. To be a bit afraid is healthy. It compels you to deal with some fundamentals.

I had a couple as clients, John and Mary, who retired in 2007 and came to me the following year, right after the market drop. John had amassed about a million dollars in his retirement account. They knew that they were going to have to take money out of that retirement account every year to live on. They felt they could pull out $50,000 a year and, with their Social Security, have a comfortable life. During the market collapse, they kept investing the same way they had in the past. They changed nothing in their retirement portfolio, and suddenly it totaled only $600,000. They were panicking, worried that they wouldn't have enough to live on.

They came in for a review, and we looked at how they were investing. They were using growth tools to generate income. They were paying more in taxes than they needed to pay. They had not protected their assets from catastrophic illness for either of them. They had an outdated will. They were set up to force all their assets to go through probate and be subject to estate tax. They hadn't established powers of attorney for financial affairs or for health care, and they had no living-will documents. They hadn't talked about a continuity plan if a source of income stopped for one of them. They had never thought about a lot of those things, and it was quite eye-opening for them. But it took a financial blow to force them through the process so they could pick up and go on with their lives. It need not be that way. They found themselves in straits that they could have avoided through careful planning.

I've seen many clients who didn't start prepping for retirement until just a few years prior. In that short time, they can't amass enough money to give themselves a good retirement. Going through life, they tend to just react to events rather than really focusing and putting enough away for the end goal. It's far better to plan well in advance with the help of people you trust.

It's Time to Protect

When you have reached retirement age, you have run out of time for the big turnaround. You no longer can outwait the economic cycles that you hope will restore your losses. You need to protect your assets, because if you take a financial blow at this point you may find your lifestyle diminished.

It's not as simple as you might think: "If I took a twenty percent loss this year," some people figure, "I'll be back to break-even if I can just gain twenty percent next year." Sorry. Even in the unlikely scenario that you did get that remarkable twenty percent return right after the big blow, it's not enough to get you back to where you were. A twenty percent loss on a million dollars, for example, brings you down to $800,000, after which a twenty percent gain raises your portfolio to only $960,000. The calculation shows you need a twenty-five percent return to get back to your million.

Generally, after taking a loss of ten or twenty percent, you need several years to get back to where you were. As you get older, you don't have that time to recover. When you take heavy losses in the early years of retirement, any subsequent gains are trying to pull the weight of the whole portfolio uphill, and even if those gains are healthy it's hard to overcome a significant early loss.

The truth of the matter is this: Your youthful phase of accumulation is over. You have reached the mature stage of preservation. And, primarily, that means accepting less market risk and instead focusing on reducing your taxes and other costs and fees. Seeking higher returns in the market is only one way to create wealth; the other way to put money in your pocket is to reduce expenses, and that should be your focus now in your quest for a better quality of life. It's time to weatherproof your portfolio. You've spent enough time out in the elements, praying for sunshine but running for cover, at times, from storms. Time to come in.

Consider that you may already have won the game and it's time to enjoy the victory. Why make risky plays that aren't likely to improve your lifestyle? It doesn't mean that you have to give up playing with flair. In your investments, you can still go for growth, but that should be a secondary concern, behind protection and preservation of your money. Your investment tools should primarily be safe ones, or ones that allow you to participate in market gains but shield you from market losses.

How much risk should you accept as you get closer to retirement? A lot of advisers will tell you about the Rule of 100, a way to roughly determine how much of your wealth to expose to market risk and how much to keep in safe or hybrid tools. Subtract your age from 100, the rule says, and that's the percentage you can reasonably keep in more market-risk investments. If you're 60, for example, you would want a ratio of 40 percent exposed to market risk and 60 percent invested in safe and hybrid tools. If you're 80, don't let more than a fifth or your portfolio be exposed to market risk.

There's some value to that rule. It can be a good benchmark as long as you understand there are exceptions to any rule, and those exceptions relate to one's history of investments and expectations. The ratio, however, should regularly be reviewed so that you feel reassured you're on track to preserve your money and maintain the standard of living you desire. The type of financial tools you use to reach for your goals will make a big difference.

What Are Your Dreams?

Again, at this stage of the game, your strategy must change depending on how well you have been playing and what you're up against next. You have new concerns in life, new priorities. Part of you likely feels that you have worked long and hard and don't want to let the important things in life slip by: appreciating your family, seeing the world, realizing the dreams you have long waited to fulfill. You may feel it's high time to take an inventory of those dreams, realistically assess what you have to work with, and get on with the rest of your life.

It's interesting to observe the spending patterns of new retirees. Typically, in the first few years of retirement they'll do some traveling and some of the activities they have been putting off. It's as if they want to get those things out of their system while they still have their health and the resources. Then they'll slide back into a very conservative mode, realizing that they do need to conserve those resources for all their remaining years. As they get older, they tend to travel less, often because they are less robust or have mobility issues – knee or hip problems, for example. They're less able physically and financially, and they are glad they did what they could earlier in retirement.

We discuss such matters with clients. We talk about their lifestyle and how much money it takes to create that lifestyle. We anticipate major expenses they'll have in the next five to seven years: Where do they want to travel, what will they be doing with the grandchildren, which charities will they be helping? After all, that's what retirement is all about.

Overcoming Fears

Retirees are younger than ever in body and spirit. And yet the pattern persists: After a few years of active living, they revert to a more conservative lifestyle and spending. Some might well be able to do a lot more than they do, yet fears resurface. And that comes down to not having a good game plan.

Reassurance works wonders.

When we're working with clients, we want to show them how they can create an income stream they cannot outlive. It's going to hedge for inflation, so we know you can maintain your quality of life without invading your principal. It seems like a very bold goal, but imagine the burden lifted off your shoulders if you don't need to worry about what the market is doing to your portfolio.

In these days when pensions are becoming a thing of the past, many retirees have to create their own income stream – creating their own pension plan, in effect. Only government workers and teachers seem to have pensions anymore. So a worker puts money away into a retirement plan, perhaps, and then at retirement gets a Social Security check.

Virtually nobody can live on Social Security alone, so the questions that arise include these: How do I take some of the money that I've worked so hard to accumulate and create my own income stream? Is it possible to do that so I am guaranteed the lifestyle to which I've grown accustomed? How do I keep my taxes at a minimum to enhance that income stream? How do I invest the rest of my money in growth tools so that I never have to invade the principal in my portfolio?

Here's how my conversation with a client might go:

"John, would you be interested if we showed you that you can take "x" number of dollars out of your portfolio every month for the rest of your life, and your wife's life, and never run out of money? In fact, John, you could leave this world with even more assets to pass on to your loved ones – and that's taking into account inflation and the potential for serious illness or other major contingencies. Interested?"

The response, often, is along the lines of, "Yeah, right. That's too good to be true." But it's a fundamental that we want our clients to recognize. We want that burden of fear off their shoulders so they can move forward confidently. We want their plan to work regardless of what the market may do.

If you have a good, defined game plan in place, you won't need to behave as if you're forever in a recession's grip. Otherwise, the usual happens: The fears surface. You may have been feeling fragile already, but then along comes a hip or knee issue. As time goes by and the doctor keeps fixing you up, you may even wonder if you'll live too long – longer than your money will last, thanks to the wonders and expenses of modern technology. Without a structured game plan, you are at the mercy of the fear of the unknown. But by analyzing your circumstances, with the help of a good retirement quarterback, you can dispel those fears.

To a lot of people, personal finances are boring. Obviously, some people thrive on keeping track of such things, but many others, to their peril, would rather not think about them. When they should act, they do nothing. There are consequences, of course, if that's you. At worst, your financial world could fall apart from such neglect. Even if it doesn't, you likely will feel an increasing apprehension as those worries about your future become ever harder to push away. In your ignorance, you lack the simple facts that could reassure you or compel you to action.

Don't Go It Alone

Even if you do like to work with figures and your portfolio, you need to ask yourself whether you possess the requisite skills and breadth of knowledge and experience to take advantage of everything that's available to make the most of your situation. Don't go it alone: You need a retirement quarterback who has seen your financial position many times and knows how to make the right play.

Many people simply do not like to talk about money, and many grew up in a household where you didn't talk about finances. They're hesitant to open up about such matters. It can be difficult enough to share that information with loved ones, and intimidating to let an adviser look over all their documents – their wills and trusts, their tax returns.

A professional wealth adviser takes that as a sacred responsibility. Clients often comment, "Bryon, you know more about me than anybody I've ever worked with, even my CPA and attorney." That's true. To do the job properly for the client, we need a wide range of information of various types, because they all interrelate: You can't talk about investing, for example, without talking about the tax ramifications and how your decisions will influence your distribution plan.

To do an adequate job, a wealth adviser needs to develop a rapport with clients so they develop a trust and are willing to share elements of their life they might otherwise keep hidden. That takes time.

You just have to kind of peel that onion back. Often, when clients hear about strategies used with others, they'll recognize similarities to their own needs, and that will prompt them to mention a concern. Digging a little deeper, the adviser can see that's a surface issue, with something more significant underlying it, unspoken, perhaps unrecognized. The adviser, having seen the same struggle unfold for many others, can promptly put that issue on the table and suggest options, guiding the client through advantages and disadvantages toward making better decisions.

Wealth advisers do tend to learn about private matters. A client, for example, might be adamant about leaving a large sum of money to a son but nothing to a daughter, and it all comes tumbling out: The daughter said something cruel, years ago, perhaps. Or she's in the grip of alcoholism. Or she's a profligate spender. Such feelings affect huge decisions on financial management. A wealth adviser can feel at times like a personal counselor, particularly when dealing with family issues involved in how the estate will be distributed.

What About Your Kids?

I ask outright how clients feel about each of their children: Are they good at managing their money? Are there extraordinary issues of concern for any of them – health problems, for example, or an impending or recent bankruptcy? How do you deal fairly with the family as a whole? I had a client whose four children weren't speaking to one another because of jealousies. The parents were helping one child more than the others. Most parents have a fairness doctrine, so the goal becomes equalizing what each child inherits, taking into consideration the extra help that any one child got in advance.

That's an issue that comes up frequently. They want to do right by all their children. So we look at each of the children. What if one's not good at managing money? In that case, a trust could be set up from which the child could take out only as much each year as is reported on his W2 form, in effect rewarding his or her work ethic.

You don't want your children to become trust babies, so you can set up differing means of distribution. For a child who is a good money manager, you can leave the funds less restricted; otherwise, you can set up an income stream instead, with a monthly stipend instead of a large sum to manage. He'll get the same amount in the end but won't end up like those lottery winners who years later have blown it all and then some.

For most people, distribution planning amounts to a simple will saying, in effect, "Honey, I love you, you get my stuff, and when you die too, it goes to the kids." That's the standard document that most attorneys provide. Most people are not aware of their alternatives. It's as if a light bulb comes on when you start telling them they have many options. You can protect this money from creditors. You can protect this money from in-laws. You can opt out of the estate tax system. You can do a lot of charitable giving. You can create income streams over time. You can create value statements and distribution planning that says the heir gets certain benefits only if he or she goes to college, for example.

"We can do that?" clients often ask, incredulously. Yes, you can. The first step is to get your wishes down on paper. Never mind how the attorney wants to draft the will or trust; what do you want to accomplish with your money?

How You'll Be Remembered

Charitable work and donations are other concerns that are often on retirees' minds. They want to leave a lasting mark on the world by supporting the work and values they believe in. They want to propagate those values in their children and grandchildren through the example of their volunteer work and sponsorship for important causes.

Most clients broach those issues, particularly during distribution planning. "Tell me how you want to be remembered," I say, and the clients will talk half an hour about where they want to leave their mark. That's quite telling, because it demonstrates the importance they place on it.

Having a good retirement plan allows you the freedom to focus on such matters. You shouldn't be wrapped up in worrying about whether you'll have the money to be able to dine out twice a month. In your retirement years, you should have the peace of mind that allows you to focus more on your contribution to society. Once the initial fears are out of the way and they have a retirement game plan, I see clients become much livelier and so much more giving of themselves. They're enjoying life.

Keeping An Open Mind

Most people have little exposure to the financial tools that are available in the marketplace. They are uninformed on taxes, so they end up paying more than they should. They don't understand how they can preserve their money and still get a good rate of return. They think they have to be out there hitting a home run in the market and taking big risks, unaware that they can reduce that exposure in many ways while still reaching their goals. When I explain their options, I hear "Oh, my!" and "Really??" They're grateful for this new knowledge.

Others, though, run the risk of thinking they know it all. They may indeed be winners, but, as Bear Bryant observed, those who are winners and know it are not necessarily the best players. They think they have a handle on everything, and may have done a pretty good job with their finances. But they need to realize there's always more to learn. They can always fine tune their abilities. That takes time and effort and study. If they deny that, they are not as smart as they think. These are bright people, well-read and sophisticated. If they had a brain tumor, they'd find the best neurosurgeon. They wouldn't get a scalpel and surgical textbook and go at it themselves.

There's no shame in not knowing. Good leadership calls for delegating responsibility to someone whose special skills and knowledge you need. That is a key to success: taking counsel from people who possess knowledge that you don't. It's essential to be able to trust and rely on others who have a good track record. A good leader takes decisive action based on information absorbed from multiple sources. That's an important quality for doing well in any aspect of life, particularly in finances. Keep an open mind.

Even if you are the best of the do-it-yourself money managers, you must consider something else: Who will do that managing if you die or become severely disabled in body or mind? Does your spouse know what you have been doing and your philosophies and expectations? Can he or she continue your fine work? Probably not. Sometimes I see a husband who is a financial wiz and a wife who pays the bills and runs the household but has no love of investments. She trusts her husband's judgment and depends on him – and if he's gone one day, what will she do? That's why you need a continuity plan. If you want to be the expert, so be it – but have a backup plan to protect your loved ones. Who are they going to call for help? It's essential to forge those relationships now. You must not wait till the situation forces immediate action.

Don't think that once you have reached retirement, it's too late to change course. It's never too late to begin effective planning and start dealing with your concerns. It's never too late to start focusing on tax issues, or income issues, or protecting your portfolio from excessive risk. It's never too late to consider how to most efficiently pass on your assets so that your loved ones get more of your money. Even if you're in your late 80s or 90s, you can improve your game plan.

No matter how the game may seem to be going, there's always time for a key play. You and the quarterback can finish in grand fashion, using your skills and savvy. You'll be able to do very well in retirement if you set your priorities, if you plan efficiently, and if you trust your teammates.

CHAPTER 2

LEARNING THE PLAYBOOK

Why You Need a Retirement Strategy

I magine a football team heading out to the field without ever having talked about the playbook. The coach doesn't bother reviewing any strategies, never diagrams a play – he just sends the team out to the gridiron saying, "Look, guys, I think you're pretty good; why don't you just figure it out as you go?" What would happen is about what you'd expect.

Some people go through life without much of a plan at all. Their goals are short-term. They figure out how to pay their monthly bills. They save for vacations and a car and somehow get their kids through college. They try to do their best through good times and bad, through sickness and health. They lose a job, they find another. The market sinks, they wait for it to rise.

During your working years, you have more flexibility. This is the accumulation phase, and you have time on your side. But when you get into retirement, you must have a good game plan. Every day, every week, every month, you'll be facing that defensive line coming at you, and you need a sound strategy. You'll face the IRS coming at you. You'll face probate and estate issues and Medicare and health issues, and investment issues. What will be your strategy? How will you face those tough guys?

Coaches emphasize that there's no "I" in the word "team." A team is not an individual, and if you're playing the game as an individual, as your own expert, you have a daunting responsibility to cover all those contingencies in your game plan. Yes, you may have a knack for investing. But do you know enough about tax issues? Can you navigate the complexities of distribution planning? Have you effectively planned for a catastrophic illness that could wipe you out financially? What about a continuity plan?

If you don't have a strategy, you'll be like a lone player fumbling on the field. You need your team to get the ball victoriously down to the end zone. You need to work in concert, knowing in advance how you'll handle a given situation – and together you can tackle the forces that threaten to turn you into a loser.

The Perils of Procrastination

Too many retirees procrastinate about such retirement planning. Procrastination is an expense. There's a cost to not taking action. In educational forums, I've illustrated that cost like this:

"Here's a twenty-dollar bill," I announce, holding one out to the audience. "Who wants it? Anyone?" Sometimes I am holding that bill for a couple minutes before somebody gets up and accepts the offer. "Yours to keep," I say, and the brave soul sits back down.

Then I hold up a five-dollar bill. "Who wants this one?" Invariably, several people jump up and reach for it immediately.

"That's an example," I explain, "of procrastination. When I held that first bill up, what were you thinking? That I was kidding? That you'd be embarrassed if you came up and got it? You had all those negative thoughts, but once you saw it was for real, you truly wanted in on the action, didn't you?"

I look at whoever snared the five dollars, and that person is always grinning.

"How much did you gain?" I ask.

"Five bucks – thanks!"

"No. You lost out on $15." I ask everyone else what procrastination cost them. It cost each of them $20 for not taking action.

Startling things can happen when you put things off. It's not unusual, for example, for a wealth adviser to come across outdated beneficiaries. Years ago, a woman came to us whose husband had died. She was his second wife, and they had two children together. He had a large life-insurance policy – over a million dollars – but he had forgotten to take his first wife off when they divorced. Her husband would have wanted that policy to benefit his second wife and kids, but the payout all went to the first wife, who was more than happy to accept it. That could have been avoided with a change that would have taken but ten minutes. The widow was devastated. She was a stay-at-home mom, and her husband had told her that money would maintain her lifestyle and put the kids through college. She now had to live with the consequences of her husband's procrastination. She had to go back to work and try to support the kids without any other additional revenue.

Procrastination can feel good for a while. "I deserve to just smell the flowers today," you can tell yourself, and you feel warm because it's what you don't know that's hurting you. You go through life not making decisions, but the pressures build and build until you're at crisis point. You've forgotten to change titles or beneficiary designations or update your will. You never review your investment strategy to reflect the economy or your impending retirement. And then – boom! You're overwhelmed.

Not making decisions, or postponing them, is hazardous to your finances. It can be hard to grasp until you see the alternative – such as saving several thousand dollars in taxes each year. Add up how much you have let slip away in a decade or more, and you'll get an idea of the damages. Had you done something about those losses ten years ago, that would be money in your pocket – or growing in your portfolio.

People let money fall through the cracks, and they are unaware. It's like getting a 15 yard penalty on the field. They could claim what's theirs safely and efficiently – and yet they do things the same way, year after year. In fact, I've made a guarantee to clients who have at least $250,000 in invested assets that if I can't find at least $5,000 in routine expenses and taxes that they are overpaying – through a review of their taxes, distribution plan and investment profile – I'll give them a hundred dollars for wasting their time.

Stress From Every Direction

Be wary, however, of those who will be all too eager to help you revise your game plan. Everybody has an opinion on how you should manage your life. Is that opinion valid? I've sometimes heard the front-porch mentality of "Billy Bob said it, so it's got to be true." But where did Billy Bob get that information? Myths and misconceptions lead to poor decisions, yet people fall for them. Whether it comes from a neighbor over the fence or from a talking head on television, an opinion is not a fact.

The financial wizards you hear on the talk shows don't always follow their own advice on investing. They profess one thing but do something else. And the producers stack the guests to reinforce a preconceived notion. You don't necessarily get a well-rounded picture, so you have to seek it out yourself from multiple sources – to get, as Paul Harvey would say, "the rest of the story."

If a talking head pronounces a financial tool good or bad, it's the most general of statements. In truth, it depends on how you use that tool, and how it functions in your portfolio. It's bad if you use it in the wrong situation for the wrong reason. It comes down to this: Don't follow anyone blindly.

Some people become victims of the other extreme: Google paralysis. They want to learn a bit more about a topic – a good instinct – but then they find a thousand or more articles they believe they need to read. They become overwhelmed with too much information and can't come to a good decision. They hesitate, and their goals slip further away.

Others become so intense that they sit at their computers as the market closes and repeatedly refresh their screens to see how their beloved stocks have done in the last second or two. I had a retired client who enjoyed day trading. We helped him develop a sound portfolio but set aside a sum so that he could, in effect, have fun with it. He'd sit at the computer throughout the day, and he set up alarms and alerts. If he had to leave the computer, he'd take a baby monitor with him. He'd listen for alerts even when he was mowing the grass. That's what he enjoyed – he loved the action – though most people would find that unbearably stressful.

Failure to plan leads to stress, poor organization leads to stress, micromanaging leads to stress, overdosing on the media leads to stress. The solution is to find a nice balance. With reliable counsel from a team of advisers, you can lay a foundation on which to base sound decisions.

Retirement planning can feel overwhelming. I understand that. It can involve thorny, contentious issues, and it forces one to confront one's own mortality. Yet indecision comes with a price. Time is not always your ally – not when it sweeps you along much faster than you anticipated. The adage holds true: The older you get, the faster time flies. Still, starting somewhere is better than never starting at all. Even if you haven't done some fundamentals along the way, you can fine-tune your finances and improve your situation.

Taking the Reins

Nobody can do it all alone. A maverick player won't last on the field. You need your team to win the game. Likewise, you need a team of specialists to help you win the financial game. Think of them as your offensive line that is there to protect you from getting smacked hard by taxes and probate and health issues and fees. A good leader surrounds himself with others who have expertise – and that holds true for a wise retiree.

You bring on an offensive line with training in different areas. You have a CPA. You may have an attorney that deals with probate and trust issues. You may have a tax specialist. You may have a stock-broker and investment adviser helping you to allocate your resources at the level of market risk you find appropriate. And your insurance agent's there to protect the assets that you have worked so hard to accumulate to make sure some unforeseen event won't take them away.

Each of those players has expertise within his or her particular specialty but may not be aware of what the other players are doing.

That's where you need your wealth adviser – your retirement quarterback –who has a broad understanding of the field of play and can coordinate the team effectively. Your quarterback communicates the goals to all the players and looks for the right play based on the strategies in the playbook.

A good wealth adviser knows a network of professionals in each area of specialty. He can help you look for who will serve you best. You need to shop for the right fit for you. If you walk into a Chevrolet dealership, the salesman will put his arm around you and walk you over to the Impala that he assures you would be just perfect for your needs. A Ford salesman no doubt would disagree. A good retirement quarterback helps you look at all the features and options and determine what's right for your portfolio to get securely to your destination.

You're not giving up control of your finances when working with advisers. You're taking the reins. You're being a good steward – and that means you cannot work in isolation. All decision makers must be part of the planning process. It's in the client's best interest.

Beware of Salesmen

Alone, you may have difficulty discerning who is telling you the true story. Your adviser should shield you from the salesmanship and lead you to genuine assistance. Insurance agents, attorneys, tax specialists – many of them are in essence salespeople. They work to derive revenue for their firms. They use a standard playbook. It's a trusted document that's best for them, but not necessarily for you. Even those who call themselves a "financial adviser" may be selling financial products that won't necessarily serve you best.

Any tool can be used improperly. If you whack a screw into a wall with a hammer it might stay in place long enough to keep a picture from falling. But if you use a screwdriver to fasten it, that picture will hang much more securely. Any financial tool can be misused, as well. If you use the wrong financial tool to do something it wasn't intended to do, you will run into trouble with your money.

A financial tool that gets abused a lot, for example, is the variable annuity. It may have high fees, and most of those selling it say its purpose is to guarantee an income stream that you can't outlive. They don't explain all of the rules that you have to follow to get that income stream. And what happens if you don't use it that way? Will you still have market risk? You can lose your principal while still paying a variety of fees every year. Regulators have come down hard on variable annuities, and rightfully so. A financial-products salesman could sell you a portfolio of mutual funds to do the same thing for growth as a variable annuity, but he makes more money selling you the variable annuity. Consider whether the adviser might be putting his own interests above yours when he makes a recommendation.

A lot of advisers aren't trained well enough to be able to share with you the advantages and disadvantages of a particular financial tool – for example, how it might not only work in your growth part but also from a tax standpoint and also fit in your estate planning. The adviser should be able to further your understanding of how all those elements work together before you make your decision to buy. Before you put your money in, you should have a good idea how much money you would be willing to lose and when you should take your profit off the table.

Evaluating your adviser

There are several questions you can ask to help identify whether the person across the table from you is really working in your best interest or his own.

"How do you get paid?" is a good question to start off with. If that person says, "I get paid a commission or a fee when I sell you a product or service," or "I share in the fee when we have assets under management," that's a commission person or a registered investment advisor. On the other hand, if you pay an adviser by the hour, you should be able to expect that he or she is working solely for you.

The following questions will help to differentiate whether the adviser that you're working with can competently play quarterback for you.

Are the financial tools and products in the retirement plan you recommend in my best interest? One would hope so, but find out whether the adviser adequately reviewed your personal situation to make sure that's the case. Is the adviser meeting a suitability standard or a fiduciary standard? A fiduciary standard is a much higher requirement: The recommendations must be appropriate for the client, and anyone reviewing them should be likely to conclude that. But under a suitability standard, the adviser can pitch any reasonable recommendation. For example, a broker can reasonably sell you investments in a mutual fund from a fund family that pays a higher commission. It's not necessarily best for you, but it's suitable, and the broker can pitch it.

How will the retirement plan affect my tax return and estate taxes, now and in the future? Many advisers are not trained in strategies that will assist you in reducing the taxes you may pay now or in the future. Many financial tools defer the tax owed – meaning you could be passing your tax consequences to your heirs, who may be in a higher tax bracket.

How will the investments you recommend affect the amount of income I'll be able to generate and its liquidity? Will the financial products keep pace with inflation, so I can maintain my standard of living as the cost of goods and services goes up? In an emergency, will I be able to get to my money without a problem? Will I have penalties for early withdrawal?

Is the retirement plan, and the financial tools it uses, compatible with my risk comfort level? I can't tell you how many times I've asked a new client to describe himself and I hear: "Well, I am a fairly conservative investor." But when I look at the client's investments, they are 90 or 100 percent at risk in the market. Their portfolio should balance their goals and risk comfort levels.

When I die, will the retirement plan and investment tools pass my assets down efficiently to my heirs? Will it protect them from excessive taxes, attorney's bills, fees and penalties? Or am I passing down an unfunded tax liability? If I have a tax-deferred annuity that has been growing over the years – now worth $200,000, for example, on $50,000 of contributions – how will that $150,000 tax liability be managed? What effect will that have on my kids?

What are your licenses and credentials? They are important, though sometimes credentials merely reflect that their holder has passed a test, yet still lacks real-world expertise. So you must dig deeper than just looking at whether the adviser has any three- or four-letter abbreviations after his or her name. But it does help; it shows that the person is definitely committed to higher education. Licensing is an important consideration for sales of securities, insurances and other products.

Learning More About Your Adviser

You can learn about a prospective adviser's licensing on various websites. Depending upon the licenses they hold, you may check with these sources: www.finra.org/brokercheck (Financial Industry Regulatory Authority) Broker Check® is a website to help investors research the backgrounds of registered representatives associated with broker-dealers. Those who hold securities licenses are required to publicly disclose information about their personal background, business background and disciplinary history. If they hold a life insurance license, you can check with www.insurance.ohio.gov (Ohio Department of Insurance). If they are licensed as a registered investment advisor, then the Security and Exchange Commission website (www.adviser.info.sec.gov) is a good resource that discloses the services provided and how they manage assets. You can learn from these sites, whether they have been censured or had complaints registered against them and find out other background information.

You may wish to check with the Better Business Bureau in your state to review consumer complaints relating to the organization or person. In addition, the National Ethics Association (www.ethicscheck.com) conducts additional background checks to make sure that the adviser truly meets high standards, listing his or her professional organizations. Does the adviser, in other words, associate with others with expertise, learning new ideas and concepts?

It's important to interview several prospective advisers as you identify those who will be good for you and your portfolio. You don't want to just go to the first person who offers a seminar or puts out a mailing. Take the time to be sure that the adviser has been down this road many, many times. You don't want to be a guinea pig. A good question to ask: "Do other professionals recommend you?" Professionals are very careful to whom they send referrals.

It comes down to this: You can't hire a financial adviser on the basis of a handshake and a smile. Background research is important, and you also should ask for references.

Developing a Rapport

In another sense, though, the handshake and a nice smile are important: A rapport has to develop, or you will need to consider switching to another adviser.

Any wealth adviser who has been in the business awhile understands that people feel apprehensive when they first come in. "Should I really disclose all my information to this person?" they wonder. They feel financially naked. It's like that awkward feeling some folks get the first time they undress for a doctor to get a physical. That feeling doesn't last. The doctor is only interested in your health, though his probing may feel uncomfortable and a bit embarrassing. And a wealth adviser is only interested in the health of your portfolio and retirement goals and dreams. That's why you need what amounts to a financial physical. The adviser needs to examine what you have been doing in your financial life and why. What are your goals? What needs to be fine-tuned? The adviser must probe, too, though in a different way than the doctor, presumably.

A doctor takes a medical history before venturing a diagnosis. A good wealth adviser must take a history, too. If you told your doctor that you had pains shooting down your side, how would you feel if the doctor responded, "Well, I bet you have an appendix in there, let's go in and take it out"? You'd expect a bit more fact-gathering, wouldn't you? Your other health conditions would play a key role in whether surgery was indicated, and such a doddering doctor could do far more harm by taking action blindly. You don't want your doctor to take just a little bit of information and run with it. You don't want your wealth adviser to do that, either.

For that information to flow smoothly, you and your adviser need to be in tune with each other. You'll hear something like this from a good adviser: "Mr. Jones, here's the goal we're trying to accomplish. Here are three options for you to consider. Here are their advantages and here are their disadvantages, and here's how this would affect your tax return, your investments, and your distribution plan." That way, you have all the information to make a very good decision. A good adviser will guide you through that process without dictating what to do but suggesting how you can reach your goals securely, and then your adviser will monitor that game plan and suggest changes as necessary.

In our firm, after we have implemented a good game plan with a client, we want face-to-face meetings twice a year because invariably we need to fine-tune the plan. Life throws some wobbly balls, and just as football players huddle on the field, so must those who influence how your finances play out. The adviser, the client, and the specialists need to work together. Sometimes a meeting of several advisers might be necessary. You may have the CPA, tax specialist, attorney, wealth adviser and the client together in a room talking about a strategy that requires the expertise of each. It's all for the good of the game.

Also, we want to include in discussions anyone who helps with financial decisions. A retired couple's adult children are commonly included and should be involved in the planning process start to finish. As the couple ages, the children commonly become increasingly involved. Everyone must be on the same page – and not just for estate planning. The couple may go to their son or daughter to talk about which investment tools they should use. The appropriate tools for mom and dad are far different than the appropriate tools for the children, and we want to make sure that's clear to all. Do they know the difference between accumulation strategies and preservation strategies? We're there to make sure.

We recommend family meetings with our clients so that we can share with the children what we do and why – and how that planning will benefit the children. We become the children's point person if something goes awry: They know we have a handle on the assets and how they are managed and organized. If one of their parents dies, they feel reassured that a continuity plan is in place to maintain the survivor's lifestyle.

Getting organized

Laying the groundwork helps immensely. Where do you keep your important papers? Where is the documentation for your assets – the deed for that property in Florida, the annual statements for those shares in XYZ Corp.? You will rest easier knowing your loved ones and advisers won't be scrambling if you die, or become disabled, or if Alzheimer's strikes.

I have had many cases in which a client has died – sometimes suddenly, as in a car crash, or a heart attack – and loved ones have to step in and continue making the financial decisions. Where's the money coming from, where's it going, what are the assets? It can be a nightmare if there's a lack of organization. If the deceased kept to himself or herself and didn't share financial information, the executor of the estate has a tough task – digging through books and records and file cabinets and figuring out where the documentation is filed or whether it even exists.

How much better to have clear and organized records that spell it all out: Here is a list of my assets, my accounts, my advisers. Here are the contact numbers of the team members who know about my finances and can carry on with the game plan.

Crucial documents that clients should bring to their first meeting include their tax return, because taxes invariably are a major issue. People want to make sure that they are not paying more than their fair share. We want to look at all of the brokerage accounts and the investments themselves, whether they are retirement or non-retirement accounts. We want to see which financial tools they are currently using. Do they have annuities? Life insurance or long-term-care policies? We want to look at those. We want to look at their powers of attorney for health care and financial, and their living-will documents along with their will or trust. All of those documents fit together to create a picture of what the client has been doing financially. We'll talk about other aspects of their finances and assets, as well, to determine if what they are doing is really helping them reach their goals and dreams in retirement.

It's important to keep your documents in a well-organized file. If you have been lax in that regard, you're not alone, but it's high time to get started. Start with the most current statements that you have. You may not be able to get all the past ones together, but take the statements as they are coming in and start organizing them. And then slowly start going back: "Okay, I know I did an investment with XYZ company three years ago, let me see if I can find those papers." We can pick up information at year-end tax time, because we might see an account that had been forgotten but that is throwing off a 1099 dividend statement or an interest statement. Year-end summaries and documents give us valuable guidance. Sometimes we need to trace the trail backwards to get a complete picture.

As for where to keep those papers, people's preferences vary. Some keep them in the house, perhaps in a secure lock box or in a fireproof box. Others keep them with their wealth adviser; others place them in a bank box. The files need to be convenient so that you can regularly update them, adding and discarding papers. And you need to let important people know where your file is located – "It's all in my safety deposit box at the bank," for example, or "It's all in this fireproof box that I've got up in the attic" or "You'll find it in my bottom desk drawer."

You want to also have multiple copies. You should create a summary document that lists your assets and accounts, with addresses and other contact information, that tells where the specific papers are located. Give that summary document to your spouse. Give it to your wealth adviser. Give it to your tax adviser or your attorney – to professionals you trust. With legal documents, you usually have two sets of originals created, one for the attorney's records and one for yours. We always keep copies of documents from our clients, we scan them, we encrypt them, and then we have them as a fallback in case nobody else can find them.

There are many variations on keeping a good filing system, but in general, the more organized you can make it, the more detailed and up to date, the better it's going to be in case someone has to step in during an emergency and pick up the pieces. Whoever that is will know what to look for and where. The better job you do at keeping comprehensive, up-to-date information, the easier that person's job will be.

If you depend on financial institutions to save your documents and statements electronically, you should also make screen prints regularly or save copies of the files to your computer's hard drive, backing them up regularly. Banks and other financial institutions generally keep those records for a limited time only – a year or two is common. Could you go back and get archived records from the bank? Yes. Will you have to pay a fee for that? Yes. So instead, why not scan the year-end statement and put it in a file of your personal finances for the year. That way you have your own record that's separate from the vendor's database.

Goals for a Lifetime

Another important paper that you would be wise to keep on file is a list of your goals and priorities. Try to keep it to one or two pages, but write down what is most important to you for the remainder of your life. How would you like to be remembered for posterity? Ask yourself these questions: "What is important to me? What do I want to be remembered for? What values do I embrace? If I were reading my obituary today, what would I want it to say about me?" Such questions get to the heart of your value system and your life goals.

Most of us have some goals in mind, but we suffer from the human foibles of procrastination and disorganization. But in your finances, failure to be organized can have serious consequences. You need to thoroughly analyze the basics – your assets, liabilities, cash flow, and protections. And you need to always keep in mind the big picture – your goals for you, your family, and posterity.

Why write those down? Because it helps to make you account-able to yourself and to others. Taking the time to make a list increases the likelihood that you'll grasp your priorities. It's been shown over and over again: People who write down their goals are more likely to accomplish them, simply because they feel accountable. When you share your goals with others who care about you, you're even more likely to succeed. You've told others what you plan to do – and that's a major incentive toward making it real.

CHAPTER 3

How to "Score 6" for the Big Win

An Income You Can Count On

The stadium is exploding in excitement, with all eyes on the end zone. The player with the pigskin races to the goal line, his opponents in hot pursuit. Perhaps he has to twist and dodge in those final yards. Maybe he has to muscle his way for every last inch of gain. But he makes it – score six!

You can be sure, as you head into your own end zone, that you, too, will face some players of fleet foot or brawny build who seem to be out to do you in before you reach that goal line. You can fend them off with some good strategies and skills as you make those touchdowns. That's where you're likely to score the most points for the big win. We're rooting for you.

When establishing your goals and dreams for your retirement, it's important to make sure that they match the reality of your finances, and sometimes that isn't the case. It comes down to knowing how you're going to maintain the lifestyle that you're accustomed to, and knowing that you will have enough money for the rest of your life. You can have all the dreams you want, but your income needs to support them. You cannot travel the world on Social Security income alone – your dream doesn't match reality. You have to make the most of what you have, using it as efficiently as possible. The smaller your bucket of money, the less you can afford a mistake, and the more you need a good qualified quarterback to help you make your plays.

Most people have done a pretty good job of accumulating assets, because they knew that in retirement they were going to have to create their own income. They knew they were going to have to generate their own pension fund, if you think of it that way. Most retirees who have plans such as 401(k)s don't have a guaranteed pension coming in, the way their parents did. Most corporations have done away with those.

That's why we must ask ourselves which types of strategies will help us to generate the income that we need for our expenses and our dreams. Through careful planning, you can know that you'll be able to account for inflation and have enough for the rest of your life. You could get to the point where you never invade your principal, so that your assets just keep growing.

That's what it means to "score six" for your retirement. It's getting to that point where you can have that lifelong, guaranteed income stream that hedges for inflation and keeps you from being tackled. You can defend against fees and taxes and market losses and the like, and you're ready for contingencies so that come what may, you won't run out of money. You feel confident that you can do all the things you want to do and spend time with the people you want to be with. You can visit the children and grandchildren. You can support the charities you believe in. You can have a good quality of life, without financial stress. Scoring the sixes gets you to that point in life where financial fears have been lifted.

Will You Live Too Long?

One of the things that people assess as they think about their aspirations is the quality of their current health. In general, people are living much longer, and that has had huge implications for the government's financial planning. Case in point: our Social Security system.

When Social Security was enacted in 1936, taking effect the next year, it set up a way to take money from workers so that it could be distributed to those no longer working. Workers contributed to the fund year after year, with the government holding the money. The idea was that once you reached your normal retirement age of 65, you would start receiving a retirement paycheck from the government for as long as you lived.

At that time, the life expectancy was 56.6 for men and 60.6 for women (source http://demog.berkeley.edu/~andrew/1918/figure2.html). It was expected that most people would retire at age 65 and die within a few years. But in the decades since, medical technology has improved so much that we're now curing what used to kill us. The life expectancy has risen to 75.7 for men and 80.8 for women (source http://www.census.gov/compendia/statab/2012/tables/12s0104.pdf), and many retirees of course live much longer. For many people, retirement means the prospect of needing thirty or more years of income without an employment paycheck. Once, you only had to prepare for several years.

The government has had to face this, and you must face it, too: You're probably going to live longer, or your spouse may live longer, and you need to provide for that possibility. You want to make sure you have enough income to let you live comfortably in the lifestyle that you're accustomed to for the rest of your life. And that raises the fundamental question: How can I do this without invading the principal of my savings? How much will I need? People don't know.

How Much Will You Need?

One of the first things to be considered is the type of lifestyle you desire during retirement – and whether you can support it. Usually in the first few months of retirement, the answer isn't clear because people are adjusting to the reality of no longer having an employment paycheck. They're trying to get a feel for which expenses are going to continue and which are going to go away or be onetime costs. Frequently, they are eager to take that big trip they have put off so many years, so we'll try to set aside money for that so they can realize that dream.

But then comes the big question of what kind of lifestyle is reasonable to expect. How much money do you need to put away for emergencies? Will you have a major expense that comes up in the next four to six years? A new roof or a new car, perhaps – where are you going to get that money? And there's the big unknown of health: Will you need long-term care? How will you deal with a severe medical condition if it arises?

As we discuss such matters, we can put numbers to most of them, thereby helping to determine how much income you will need to maintain your chosen lifestyle. Once you know how much you will need for daily expenses, for contingencies, and to pursue your dreams, it's time to craft an action plan. But how?

Secure Streams of Income

Back in the Jimmy Carter years, when interest rates were 12 or 13 percent, you could take a $100,000 Certificate of Deposit and have it throw off $12,000 to live on. Recently, that CD would have been throwing off $1,000 or $2,000 of income. So clearly you need to find a better way to survive.

However, subjecting your finances to market risks is not the answer. A soaring economy can turn into a flagging one, as we all know too well, and it's hard to change your lifestyle to adapt. That's why it's a mistake to have money at risk in the market when you're using it for income. If you're pulling money out while the market is falling, you cannot recover quickly enough.

In creating a retirement plan, we look at different financial tools that can create an income that you cannot outlive. At this stage in life, as we have seen, it just won't do to allow your income to be subject to any market fluctuation. Depending on how much you need for the lifestyle you want, your retirement portfolio will have a combination of income and growth tools.

In assessing those financial tools for a retirement plan, we look at which ones are most appropriate for different periods of time. You may have a financial tool, for example, that's very good for generating income in the first five years of your retirement. Meanwhile, another tool sits and grows untapped for the first five years, then generates an income stream for the sixth through tenth years of your retirement.

You can keep a third financial tool growing for those first ten years and then it can be your income source for the ensuing decade.

That way, regardless of whether the market rises or falls, you will be using the right kind of tool to create the income stream when you need it. And by selecting the proper group of financial tools, you can make sure that your income is tax-efficient. For example, you might have an income source of $2,000 per month that's only taxed as if it were $300. That's a major factor in making your money go further.

If you have other income from sources – such as dividend and interest income from investments, or capital gains from the sale of securities – I usually will take those off the table because they can fluctuate in value from year to year. For peace of mind, retirees need to know their lifestyle is secure. No matter what happens on Wall Street, they need to know their check will still be coming in reliably, and they can do all the things they'd hoped to do.

Right Tool for the Right Job

You want to use the financial tool that's specifically designed to accomplish your retirement goal. If you need income, then we want to focus on tools that will throw off guaranteed streams of income on a tax-advantaged basis. If we're looking for growth, then we want to look for very good long-term growth tools that also offer a tax advantage. You don't want to take a growth tool and have it throw off income, because then it doesn't grow efficiently and it causes you to pay more in taxes than you should. We need to review the different types of guarantees that may back up the financial tool that is used. CD's may be FDIC insured. A bond guarantee will vary with the issuer (US government, state, municipality, corporate, etc.).

The guarantee of an annuity is backed by the financial strength of the underlying insurance company.

The first step in working with a client is to find out how close we can get to the lifestyle and goals desired. Is that lifestyle realistic? Often we can show clients that, yes, they can maintain the lifestyle they have grown accustomed to, and yes, we can allocate part of their investable assets so they create an income stream. We may use several tools to accomplish those income needs during their retirement years. A structured income plan is a typical component of many retirement plans. Some people may use a laddered CD approach or a bond portfolio; others may use an annuity payout system to create the guaranteed income.

Once we have guaranteed the income needs, the remaining investable assets will be focused on growth. The goal is to use financial tools in each of three categories to grow the assets in such a way as to replenish the income over time. If we accomplish that goal, the retiree's principal will never be invaded.

Tools for Safety, Growth, or Both

Every financial tool will fit into one of three categories. It may be a safe, hybrid, or market-risk tool, and you should consider having some of your growth money in each of these categories. Let's take a look at each.

Safe tools will consist of CDs, savings accounts, money markets, fixed annuities and U.S. government-backed bonds. With these financial tools you have safety of your principal, and you can get to these monies easily. However, your return in this category is very modest and may not keep up with inflation.

Market-risk tools may include stocks, bonds, mutual funds, unit investment trusts, variable annuities, REITs, etc. These tools have unlimited upside potential but also have the potential to lose your principal. This is the world of Wall Street. It's where most people have been playing on the accumulation side.

Hybrid tools try to take the strength of safe and market-risk tools and bring their advantages together. The intent is to allow your money to participate in some of the growth of the market but never the losses of the market. In this category you have equity-linked CDs and equity-linked fixed annuities.

By allocating a different percentage of monies into each of these categories – safe, hybrid and market risk – you can get a balanced return. Let's say I allocated a third of my growth money into each category. If the market goes up, all three areas grow. If the market goes down, only one area will drop in value, which is the market risk money. The other two-thirds still will be making money or staying the same.

So it's a balancing act between those three categories and then choosing the right type of financial tool within each category that will help reach the goal as safely and securely as possible. To have an efficient investment game plan in retirement, you will use different tools in each of those categories for a growth and income strategy.

A lot of times, investors don't keep in step with their portfolios, and they end up taking a lot more risk than they intended. They make decisions based on growth and accumulation, but they never move into the preservation phase. They may have excessive concentration in a particular stock or a particular industry sector because it worked well for them in the past and they became comfortable with it.

When considering how to rebalance and allocate assets, you first have to look at the type of financial tools you are using and where they fit.

Every financial tool has two of three fundamental characteristics, which are growth, liquidity, and safety. In the market risk side, we have growth and we have liquidity but we give up safety. In the safe side, we have safety and we have liquidity, but we give up growth. In the hybrid side, you have some growth because you participate in market gains to an extent; you have safety because your principal is protected from market losses; but you give up more liquidity.

Whether those characteristics are good or bad for you depend on how you are using each tool. You first have to look at the big picture. If you have 95 percent of your portfolio over on the market risk side, do you feel comfortable? Could you face going through another market downturn and loose a large percent of your account value? What effect would that have on your retirement game plan?

It's likely you'll decide to move some assets over to the hybrid or the safe side, balancing your portfolio. Once you have done that, then you can consider specifics of the market risk side, such as which sectors to invest in. Do you want to be ultraconservative? Do you want to be very aggressive? Large cap, small cap, mid cap? Do you want to be sector-oriented, such as in tech and utilities?

However, you have to start with the big picture: You have to step back and look at the overall game plan first and decide how to allocate your investable assets by the three categories of risk, safety, and hybrid. Do you have enough liquid money, safely allocated for your income needs? Or do you perhaps have too much money that's safe and liquid, thereby sacrificing growth opportunity?

In other words, focus first on what ultimately will get you to the goal line, not on how you can grab a yard or two on the field of play. After you clearly grasp an overall strategy, then you can work out the details.

Rebalancing

As the years go by, you need to monitor whether your investment style still matches your needs and goals. If your game plan was set up at age 50, how did your goals then compare with those you have now at age 65? What will they be at 85? You need to adjust your portfolio accordingly as the years pass.

Check regularly to make sure performance is sufficient and you're getting the rates of return you want, that you have enough safety and liquidity and the right growth. You must also consider whether your goals and objectives are changing. Is anything going on in your life that would call for more liquidity? Do you need to make some changes in your overall goals?

Once you have determined sensible ratios of risk and safety, you and your adviser need to monitor your portfolio and make some short-term modifications. The year-to-year gains and losses on the various aspects of your portfolio will result in a changing ratio of safety vs. risk in your total portfolio, and you will have to go back and rebalance. As the market ebbs and flows, you'll make some small adjustments accordingly.

In rebalancing, you take some profit off the table so that you can stay very close to the original ratios you established. Let's say you have a great growth year: There's nothing wrong with taking part of the profit from your top-growing assets off the table and investing it elsewhere for better growth opportunity. Again, the principle is that you want to buy low and sell high – not the opposite, as most investors do.

As an example, if you are just doing a stock to bond ratio, you might be able to buy bonds at a discount. Then, when bonds do well, you can take some of that profit off to buy more equities at a lower value. In theory you are first buying underperforming bonds, waiting for them to perform well, selling them at their high point, and using that growth profit to buy equities when stocks are down.

It seems like a lot of work to monitor your assets sufficiently. And that's why you need a good wealth adviser. You need the quarterback who can help you make decisions and guide you through the plays.

Bonds and Stocks: Both Spell Risk

In considering whether your portfolio has the proper risk ratio of safety and growth, you may feel you took care of those percentages long ago. You established what you felt was a wise mix of stocks and bonds. That seemed to be the prevailing advice.

However, most bonds are not safe. Most bonds are in the market risk side. The only bonds that are safe are the ones that are government-backed such as Treasuries and Ginnie and Fannie Mae and Freddie Mac bonds. Those are the ones that have the safety feature to them. Corporate or municipal bonds are not considered safe tools. Many people who are in bonds are in funds, not owning individual bonds. With an individual bond, the only way to know it is really a safe tool is if you are certain you will never sell it through the whole term of that bond. If I am buying a ten-year bond with XYZ Corporation, that corporation may stop paying dividends, and may ultimately default on the bond. So there is some risk involved there, yet I have to know that I am going to be in that bond for the duration.

It's true that bonds are less risky than other types of financial tools. But it's not avoiding all risk. If your portfolio lacks sufficient liquidity and a health-care issue comes along, what kind of a discount would you face if you were to sell those bonds? How much of a loss would you have to take? Perhaps your decision on the percentage to keep in bonds was once a good one, but as you have gotten older, is that still the case? Or do you have less risk tolerance?

The "Buy, Hold, and Hope" Myth

Some clients feel that the best policy is not to mess too much with finances – that the wise policy is to buy, hold, and hope. You buy it, you hold it, you never let go of it, hoping it does well. That may have worked twenty or thirty years ago, but today it doesn't. The market is moving so much faster and is so much more volatile.

To understand the thought process of buy and hold, consider a stock that goes from $20 a share, up to $88 a share, then down to 56 cents a share – all in 18 months. When the stock is on the way up, as an investor, you're bragging, "Man, I picked a great one." And you're just happy as a lark to see it at $88. And then it drops to $60. "Well, you know, geez, it's just a market correction, not a big deal," you tell yourself. Then it's at $40. "Hey, I've still doubled my money." Then you're back to break-even. "Hey, I know the market's just ready to turn around. Let's just hang in there for a little longer." Oops, it's down to $10 a share. "The market has to go up sometime, like the broker keeps saying, so I'll hang in there, and things will get better." And at 56 cents a share, you figure you can't afford to sell.

If, say, nine years later, that stock is trading all the way up at $3.25 a share, how long do you think you'd need to hold it just to break even again at $20 a share? You'd be better off in a savings account. I call it the buy, hold and hope strategy. It's just hoping you'll win. It's an outdated style of investment in our changed economy. You have to be a good steward. You can't just be an ostrich with your head in the sand. You always need to make sure that you know what's going on in the market and know how your investments are doing compared with industry benchmarks.

An Exit Strategy

When you invest, you want to play the game to win. You want a return on your money – but inherent in that effort is the amount of risk you take. You may recall that old Will Rogers quote: "Before I worry about a return *on* my money, I want to make sure I get a return *of* my money." So the first principle in preservation is, "Will I get my money back?" The second is, "What kind of rate of return can I expect on this?" We want to keep score.

One of the ways to keep score in the market is to have benchmarks so you know how you are doing. Am I making money or losing money? How am I doing compared to an industry benchmark? If I don't keep score and I don't use a benchmark, it's kind of like playing football and not keeping score. We all have a good time but we don't know whether we won or lost. In investing, you want to keep score and win.

You want to have benchmarks that tell you, for example, whether a three percent return on your portfolio this year was better than average. Well, if the average index did two, then you did better. But if the average index did five, you didn't do very well. You may like your three percent, but in truth you actually did a lot worse than the market – and when you consider all the fees and taxes that you had to pay to get that three, did you really come out ahead? So you have to keep score, and you need a way to judge how you're doing so that you can take corrective actions as the market changes.

You also want to have an exit strategy, which amounts to this: "When do I sell? How much profit do I think I can make? And when I get there, am I willing to take it off the table?" Are you willing to sell when you have made X percent on the investment and move on to the next opportunity, even if you have to pay some tax? Will you know when you have accomplished your goal for the investment?

Even more important, an exit strategy must include another question: "How much am I willing to lose on this investment?" Most people do a very good job of identifying why they want to buy – whether it is Procter & Gamble, IBM, or Apple – but then they need to make two pledges to themselves before they buy. "When I've reached my goal and made what I expected, I will get out." And the second crucial consideration: "If it goes down 10 percent (or 15 percent, or 20 percent), I am done. I am not going to lose any more than that."

In retirement, this is critical: Preservation of principal becomes very, very important. Without these two questions, you're just playing the game and not keeping score. It's like gambling without any self-control. You need to know when to hold 'em and know when to fold 'em. Know how much you're willing to lose, and how much is enough to win. Otherwise you get into trouble.

Every financial tool is going to have a time when it is very, very good. But that same financial tool will go through some cycles when it's not very good. And the market isn't logical about anything. So if I am buying XYZ stock, as an example, it may have a ten-year run-up. Then, if it starts to decline, there's nothing wrong with taking my profit off the table. In the earlier example, that investor could have sold out at $65 instead of running it all up to $88. Then, after the stock plunged to 56 cents and began rising, he could buy it back again. Nothing wrong with that at all.

But most people aren't disciplined. They buy by emotion. They don't think it through by asking themselves, "Why do I want to buy this? How much do I think I can make? How much do I think I can lose?" They don't keep score. They play the game, and they enjoy the ups and downs of the roller-coaster ride, but they never know whether they are actually getting ahead.

A recent DALBAR study said that over the last 20 years a typical investor made about a 3.8 percent return on his money (www.dalbar.com 2011 study). That's pathetic. Most people, when the market is going down, wait till it goes close to the bottom. Consider that investor whose stock fell to 56 cents. Let's say he finally pulls the trigger and says, "Okay, I am done." He bought it at $20 but sells it at 56 cents. And then he'll wait until the market corrects again and now the market proves that it's in a growth cycle, and then he'll go back in. And maybe he buys it at $20 again. That's the typical investor. They'll buy high and sell low, because they are basing their decisions on misinformation and emotions. That's why you need an exit strategy to preserve and protect your investment dollars.

Overconcentration

Overconcentration in the market is a major risk that all investors must avoid. Some investors with million dollar portfolios lost half that value in 2008 because their wealth was concentrated in market risk, whether in individual stocks or sectors. If they had planned to retire and take out five percent for income, their financial picture changed dramatically. You can imagine how they felt. Could they still retire on the limited funds? Could they hope for a recovery of their losses?

If you are depending on an income from money you have concentrated in market risk, you are asking for trouble. You are likely to find yourself withdrawing money from a falling account. It's not your money you're compounding – it's your problems.

Diversification is the answer. Many people have much of their wealth in their company's stock. Look at the employees of Enron who bought company stock and suddenly found out the company books were altered and saw the value of that stock plunge to nothing. Don't make a similar mistake.

People sometimes fall in love with specific investments. And, unfortunately, the investment doesn't love you back. Every investment tool will have times when it does very, very well. But it'll also have times when it doesn't perform very well at all. To buy, hold and hope is a risky ride. It's good, of course, to ride uphill, but it's wise to take some of that profit off the table before it goes down. You can revisit the investment after it begins the next growth phase.

Overconcentration isn't necessarily in a specific equity. It can be in a sector. Government regulation can take an industry from top-notch to the bottom. Outside forces come into play. Global issues come into play. If you have too much concentration in a specific country and then all of a sudden there's some sort of war or insurrection there, your stocks take a bath. Why would you take such a risk with your portfolio when you need it for retirement income and want to pass assets to your children?

Think of it this way: You constantly have to change your plays. You have running plays, you have passing plays, you have end runs, and you have some trick plays. You want to use different strategies to get you safely down the field with the ball, free of interceptions.

If your strategy leaves you at risk, some opponent or another is likely to tackle you.

Hedging for Inflation

One of those players that could tackle you is inflation. Consider whether your financial plan has the flexibility to deal with the effects of rising prices. Will you be able to adjust?

You can't just assume that if you have an income stream today of X, and a lifestyle today of Y, that through life it's going to be that same way. In the early years of retirement, most people spend more because they are doing the things that they have put off until retirement. Then after five or ten years in retirement, they slow down and focus on the kids and family. They don't travel as much. Their lifestyle is more modest.

Expenses, however, might still increase. You need to hedge to make sure that even though your lifestyle now may be slower, in the future it may cost you more dollars and you need to make sure your investments can stay up with inflation or actually exceed inflation. You need to consider the true growth that you got from your invest-ment portfolio. If inflation was three percent last year, and you got a three percent return, you didn't get any growth at all. You have to look at the effect of inflation on your portfolio. Not all that long ago, gasoline was 25 cents a gallon, and look at it today.

Investment Fees and Tax Issues

Most people don't know what they are paying in fees for a specific investment, and they may be vague about the tax consequences. They look at the gross return on their investment, but it's rare they fully consider the net return. Will fees and expenses take that performance down? Do you have to pay tax on these investments, either now or later? What ramification does that have on your rate of return?

The investor may have considered the fees when he first set up the account but doesn't pause later to realize that the real winner seems to be the fund manager who is consistently taking out his cut—or Uncle Sam—who also seems to be making out very well. You get the feeling "they are winning and I am losing."

Most financial tools hide the fees. Mutual funds usually disclose two of the five fees that are applicable to that tool. So, you look at the 12b-1 fee and the M&E, the maintenance and expense fee, and you think you understand the fees associated with the tool, but actually three more fees are involved. You have to look at all of them.

There are hidden fees in financial tools like variable annuities. They can be very expensive. The company discloses them, but most people never read the prospectus. You can have between two and four percent in fees in this tool each and every year. Think about that: Your investments could have to make a four percent rate of return just to deliver a zero return to you.

How do you find out about fees? You should start with the prospectus, though it's not exactly light reading. The prospectus discloses all the fees. It's extremely important information and highly detailed. How else could you get information? Some of it you can get in the public domain through Morningstar or Thomson Financial, or you can go to Yahoo Finance or similar sites. You can get some of the information, but it's not as detailed and it's not the full story. It's only part of the story. An expert in that area has access to research and analysis tools and can tell you not only the fees involved in a mutual fund but also exactly, as of last night, what stocks were in that portfolio. You get a lot more detail than what's out in the public domain.

Once you consider the fees, expenses and tax ramifications, you can calculate your net return. Then you can compare it with indurstry benchmarks. For example, a modest-growth mutual fund is likely to be benchmarked to the S&P 500. So if I am in a mutual fund and that mutual fund manager is charging me 1.5 percent per year to make those management decisions, wouldn't it be reasonable for me to expect that my investment should do better than average? You want to make sure that, after the fees, you're doing better than what you can do without paying those fees. The industry average is like getting a "C" in school. Don't you want a "B" or an "A" in your portfolio?

You also want to consider whether you are in the best tool for the category. Let's say, for example, that you're in a growth mutual fund. You can compare it with other mutual funds that are managed the same way – its peer group. How does your money manager fare when compared with 500 others who manage the same way? Is he in the top 10 percent or bottom 10 percent? Or evaluate a stock according to its sector. Is it the best in the sector? All of those things come into play to determine what type of financial tool would be most appropriate in any particular category.

You might also do a web search to find information about the manager. If you're using a mutual fund, as an example, look at how long the manager has been on the job. The average life expectancy of a money manager in a mutual fund is less than four years. If your money manager has been on the job for three years, you can't look at the five-year, the ten-year, and the fifteen-year history of that fund because he didn't create that return. You can only consider the three- and one-year returns.

Your wealth adviser can help you weigh the fees, taxes, and relative performances, making sure such investments are appropriate for your retirement plan. He can help you consider investments you might have overlooked, and he can help you keep a good perspective.

For example, I had a client years ago who was adamant about investing in "no-load" mutual funds. His expenses were indeed very low, totaling about three-quarters of a percent, around 0.6 to 0.81. But by placing such emphasis on the no-load aspect, he was ruling out options that could have served him well. To demonstrate, I showed him the best-performing no-load fund. Its net, over ten years, averaged 14 percent.

"Now, let's look at a loaded fund," I told him. "Here's one you'd never consider, but over ten years it grossed 24 percent. Yes, it had three percent in fees for the money manager, but still, that's a 21 percent net return. And you would never have found this fund because you're so focused on the load. It's an important consideration, but it's just one component of many." You have to consider fees, but you also have to look at the money manager's performance record and the tax consequences. Isn't it what you get to keep that's the most important?

Scoring Six: A Strategy in Action

When you find yourself scoring sixes, you gain the confidence that you are winning the game. You feel reassured that you will not run out of money and can live the way you want through your retirement years. You have hedged for inflation. You have kept taxation at bay. You have anticipated health-care issues and other contingencies, while making sure you have enough reliable income to live well.

To get there, you will balance a variety of financial tools that are safe, hybrid, and market risk. Together these will produce the income stream that lasts through your retirement, keeping up with inflation. The portion of your money that can be devoted to growth tools is also balanced, so that some of it is relatively safe while other assets, though exposed to the markets, provide a rate of return that keeps your principal intact and growing.

Let me give you an example to illustrate the growth and income strategy. We had a client with a little over $1,000,000 of investable assets, and we needed to create an income that he couldn't outlive that would maintain his lifestyle. We utilized several financial tools for specific periods of time. We used one tool with "x" number of dollars in it to create the stream of income for the first five years and making it very efficient from a tax standpoint.

We put another block of money in another tool designed to create an income for years six through ten. Because the money won't be needed for several years, we can invest it for a higher rate, hedging for inflation. We took a similar approach with a third block of money. It will sit for ten years, and then in year eleven it will create the income stream for the rest of his life.

In this example, we have taken about $250,000 of investable assets and moved them into the income strategy side to provide the income stream needed for their lifestyle. If they die prematurely and there is money left in these accounts, this money will pass to their heirs. That leaves the remaining $750,000 for the growth side of the equation. The question is what rate of return is needed to make sure that in ten years the total portfolio is back to a million dollars? If you run the math, you see it's about 2.92 percent. So how much risk do we have to take to make sure that we never invade your principal? Not much. We could create a stream of income for life, and in ten years the portfolio probably will be worth $1.3 million, or $1.4 million because we'll likely get a better return over those 10 years than just the 2.92 percent.

With such an investment strategy, you have time on your side even if you do take some market risk. If the market falls, that money can be left in place to recover, since it won't be needed for years, if at all.

We showed that client a way to score six. The strategy could create the lifestyle he had grown accustomed to, with a hedge for inflation. There would be no need to invade the principal, and the retiree would have a million dollars or a lot more to pass on to heirs.

When you know that these things are in place, you can enjoy retirement. You can focus on what's really important, which is quality of life, spending time with the people you love, and giving back to your community. You shouldn't be glued to your personal computer with bated breath, worrying about each stock update and your daily rates of return. Most people wouldn't call that fun. You shouldn't feel compelled to count every dime of your income. Instead, you should have an income you can count on.

CHAPTER 4

How to "Score 3" and Save on Taxes

Making Sure Your Share Is Fair

What happens in football when you get a penalty? You end up going backwards. You end up having to move back five, ten, fifteen yards, and then you need a do-over. You have to fight to regain a position that you already had. In your finances, you suffer such a setback when you pay taxes unnecessarily. If you have scored six with your financial tools and developed a sound income for your retirement, you can add to your good fortune with some extra points when you pay no more than your fair share to the tax man.

Albert Einstein was a brilliant physicist, yet he is quoted as saying: "The hardest thing in the world to understand is the income tax." Not the theory of relativity. The income tax.

But of this you can be certain: You are expected to pay your fair share and no more. Many people pay more than their fair share, but with effective tax strategies they could significantly reduce what they owe. And there's nothing wrong with that.

"There are two systems of taxation in our country: one for the informed, and one for the uninformed," said Judge Learned Hand, renowned jurist and judicial philosopher. "There is nothing sinister in so arranging one's affairs as to keep taxes as low as possible," he said, as the courts have established time and time again. "Everybody does so, rich or poor, and all do right. For nobody owes any public duty to pay more than the law demands."

You might be wise to presume yourself uninformed. The more you learn, it seems, the more you learn you don't know. Our system of taxation is so complicated, with so many rules and regulations, you could end up paying too much because you don't know what section of the code to use to pay your fair share. You need a comprehensive strategy.

Take it from former Chief Justice of the Supreme Court William Rehnquist: "There's nothing wrong with a strategy to avoid the payment of taxes. The Internal Revenue Code doesn't prevent that."

So, ultimately what we're saying here is that it's our American duty to position our finances in such a way as to pay the least amount of tax. That's what we're supposed to do. We're patriotic when we pay our fair share, not more than our fair share.

The IRS is not going to send you a thank you note because you overpaid your taxes. It is going to assume that you know what types of financial tools are in the marketplace. It assumes you understand the tax ramification of those financial tools and are intentionally using those tools for that advantage. If you believe other financial tools will help you get to your goal safer and more securely, so that you can get the same or better return with lower risk and lower tax expenses, it's okay to use those tools.

When we review tax returns, it's clear that people don't understand some of those principles. Earlier in this book, I mentioned a client who was proud of the 12 percent return his broker was getting for him. This was back in the early 2000s, right after the tech bubble. That kind of return seemed very reasonable for that time, and he'd gotten it for a couple years. But it was the gross return – he was netting 4 percent after a $10,000 tax hit. Many people who sell financial products don't have a good understanding of the tax ramifications so, in turn, they are only giving you part of the story. This particular client, for sure, wasn't considering the whole story. We were able to raise his net return to seven percent.

Because he and the broker weren't looking at the total picture, they were falsely thinking they were doing very well. That scenario happens often. The IRS wasn't about to commend him for overpaying his taxes by $10,000 every year. And over five years, he paid $50,000. Was that his fair share? Absolutely not. His fair share could have been zero, or very little. Yet, not only was he obligated to pay that $50,000, but the situation was causing the income from his pension and his Social Security to be in a higher tax bracket as well.

So it's kind of a double-edged sword. When you're not using the right type of financial tools and considering the tax ramifications, you end up paying a lot more than your fair share of taxes. And he could have put that $50,000 to such good uses – improving quality of life, enhancing dreams, or building a fund to pass on to family or people in need.

The government isn't worried about protecting the quality of your life. It's more than willing to get what it can from you and redistribute it. If you retain that $50,000, you can control who gets that money – your own favorite charities, for example, as opposed to the government's choice.

So it doesn't make sense for you to send more money to the IRS than you need to.

It's about knowledge. And having somebody knowledgeable help you understand the relationship between the financial tools that you're using and their tax consequences.

Phantom Income

Mutual funds are a good example. In non-retirement accounts, they throw off what we call phantom income. And that phantom income has no direct relationship to the account balance.

Here is an example from a prospective client. They had invested $50,000 in a mutual fund on January 1. By December 31, the account balance was down to $35,000. It was a mutual fund that he had picked on his own, and the money manager lost him $15,000 that year on paper.

But then, in mid-January of the next year, he got a 1099 statement showing he owed tax on $12,000 of gain. This gain was created from the mutual fund buying and selling investments during the year. All capital gains must be distributed to the shareholders of record each year. So even though his account lost $15,000 on paper, he had a "phantom" income of $12,000. He had to pay income tax on the $ 12,000. Did he really earn that $12,000? No. It was fictitious. But it was a very real tax burden. He does get to increase his tax basis from $50,000 to $ 62,000 so when he does sell the mutual fund, this "phantom" income will be recognized.

I don't have a problem paying tax when I make money. If my account goes from $50,000 to $75,000, I don't have any problem paying a percentage of tax on that $25,000 of growth. That's what we should do. But I do have a problem when my account goes from $50,000 down to $35,000 and I have to pay tax on $12,000. That doesn't make a lot of sense.

True, your new basis in that mutual fund is now $62,000, not the original $50,000. However, most people in their tax calculations will forget that they have already paid tax on that $12,000. They look at the original investment, see the gain, and figure they'll have to pay the tax if they liquidate it. People end up paying tax not only once but sometimes twice on some types of investment tools because they don't keep good records. And they don't understand the taxes.

Situations such as that require careful attention. Someone with knowledge of how different financial tools operate needs to consider whether, as in that example, they generate phantom income. And someone needs to monitor the portfolio to assess whether numerous other consequences could arise.

Tax-Free, Tax-Deferred

Taxable accounts are, by definition, those that are subject to ordinary income tax, whether it is on dividends, interest income, or capital gains. On an investment account that you have funded with after-tax dollars, gains will be taxable.

In a tax-deferred account, such as a 401(k) or IRA, you fund the account with pre-tax dollars, and you don't pay taxes on its growth until you take the money out of the account. You are deferring the tax to some point in the future. Annuities are also a tool that will allow you to defer the tax on the growth. Stocks are also an example of a tax-deferral account. You don't have to pay tax on the gain until you liquidate that position.

A tax-free account requires no tax on the gain. For example, a Roth IRA is funded with after-tax dollars but grows on a tax-advantage basis – meaning you're not taxed yearly on the growth, and all of the money that you withdraw from the account is 100 percent income-tax free. There are accounts that have those same three characteristics. We call them Roth look-alikes. They allow you to receive money on an after-tax basis, let it grow on a tax-advantage basis, and get the money out on a tax-free basis.

Different financial tools fit into each of those three categories, and it's important to use the right tool for the right job – the same as you need to consider which tools work best for your risk profile, as we saw in the last chapter. Which you choose will depend on what you are ultimately going to do with the money.

Keeping money in your pocket is your goal, and certain investments seem to target retirees for taxes. There are tools that are marketed as tax-free, like a triple net tax bond, meaning that I don't have to pay tax on the income at the federal, the state or the city level. Well, that's true. I don't have to pay income tax at those three levels, but it may not be 100 percent tax free for a retiree. When you compute how much of your Social Security benefit is taxable, you have to include in your calculations the interest income you earned from that "tax-free" bond. In other words, you end up forcing more of your Social Security into taxation. That's an example where tax free really isn't tax free.

Annuities

Annuities are a tax-deferral tool, allowing you to postpone payment to a later date. You don't have to pay income tax on the growth annually as you receive it as you would for a CD or an investment that pays interest income every year.

In an annuity, you get to shield that growth, but then you have to pay tax on all the gain when you take money out. That tool can work well – why pay tax on money you are not using? The deferred tax helps the account grow substantially.

Here's an example comparing the growth of a $100,000 taxable account and a $100,000 tax-deferred account, at a twelve percent rate of return over ten years. In the taxable account, you pay taxes every year on those earnings – let's say 25 percent, including federal and state tax. At the end of 10 years, you would have an account balance of $229,033. If you grew the money in a tax-deferred account over the same period and then paid 100 percent of the tax at the end of the ten years, the tax-deferred account would net $251,621.

Compare the net totals in each of the accounts. Even after you pay what you owe at the end of ten years, the tax-deferred account will always be bigger. The tax total will be higher, but because of the account's superior growth, you'll have more money to spend.

That's highly attractive, but at some point it becomes inefficient if you're not planning to use the asset and intend to pass it down to somebody else. If I don't convert that, let's say, into an income stream of some kind at some point or take that money out and pay the tax, then I am going to pass that asset down to my children – and give them the tax liability that I didn't pay. I passed it on to them.

So, if I put $50,000 into an annuity, and over ten years it grew to $200,000, now I have a $150,000 tax bill for my children. That's far from tax efficient, but it can be minimized. The retiree can decide which financial tools will do that best by reviewing the tax consequences. Annuities can be a useful financial tool. You need to be aware that if you take money out of an annuity prior to age 59 ½, you may be subject to a 10% penalty. Annuities are backed by the financial strength of the underlying insurance company.

Retirement Accounts

Retirement accounts may be one of the worst accounts to have in your portfolio, yet more retirees have them than probably anything else. They have a large IRA or a 401(k) plan that they have worked so hard to accumulate over the years and they don't realize there's a huge tax lien on it. It's not a question of *will* they pay tax on it. The question is when.

As you contribute to an IRA, you get a tax deduction. When you put money into your 401(k) plan, you are using pre-tax dollars. In both accounts, you will not pay taxes on the growth. But there will come a time when you are required to start taking money out. Every dollar that you withdraw is going to be subject to whatever tax bracket that you are in at that time. Because you are taking money out of the account, it can force other aspects of your income to be in a higher tax bracket, i.e., if I am receiving Social Security income, the withdrawal from my retirement account can force me to pay a little bit more in tax.

A retirement account is the only account that we own in which the government requires us to take money out. When we get to that magic age of 70½, we have to start taking a required minimum distribution. If you do not take the distribution, you are subject to a 50 percent penalty tax. If you take money out prior to 59½, you may be subject to a 10% penalty – in addition to paying tax on the withdrawal. The larger the account becomes, the more tax you will owe.

With retirement plans, we'll show clients a review of the tax lien on their retirement account. Let's just live in a fairytale world for a moment. Let's assume taxes do not change for the rest of your life. Let's assume that we get a below average rate of return, maybe 3 or 4 percent each year, and then we only take money from the account when we have to.

We'll show clients the minimum amount of money they will have to take out of the account during their life. Many people don't need the money or want to withdraw it. We'll show them the minimum lifelong tax that they will pay on this account. "Here is the potential balance to your heirs when they inherit it," we say. "And here is the income tax they will owe on the balance." Also, the inherited retirement account can be subject to estate taxes.

So, a retirement account is not efficient from a tax standpoint. We know we have a tax liability. The larger the account is, the more of it is Uncle Sam's and the less of it is yours. From a tax planning standpoint, we show clients ways to reduce that tax liability. Let's try to minimize that future tax liability and structure it so we either don't have to take a distribution because we moved it into a tax free environment or else we significantly reduced the tax burden. We spend a lot of time trying to develop ways to reduce the tax burden on those accounts.

Remember, the only money that you should be paying taxes on is money that you're currently using for living expenses. You may find your Social Security and pension income is enough for the lifestyle you need, but nonetheless you are required to take $10,000 or $15,000 out of the retirement account every year and pay tax on it. You don't need the money, you don't want it, but you are forced to take that distribution. And you can expect to be passing that tax liability down to your heirs.

There are many ways to reduce or even eliminate the taxes that are owed on retirement accounts. A retirement quarterback can assist you with deciding which play will be the most efficient for you.

Success Comes by Seasons

Tax efficiency in your investments is one step on the way to winning the game. As every football fan knows, true success comes by seasons, not by individual games. The coach, the owners and all involved need to look at more than a single game. They need to look at what's happening with their entire season and the years ahead as they plan which players to draft and how to move forward to the future. A good retirement coach can help to decide which players to keep from year to year and which have served their purpose.

CHAPTER 5

GOING FOR THOSE EXTRA POINTS

Leaving Assets to Loved Ones and Charities

hen I think of the football greats, I think of men who played for the love of it, not because of the money. Jim Brown, running back for the Cleveland Browns, was one of those players who meant a lot to me when I was a kid. He set record after record for Cleveland.

And I admired Joe Namath, a true icon, a champion not just on the field but in his work to get decent pay for players. I admire Mike Ditka for his Gridiron Greats foundation that provides medical and financial aid to pioneers of the game who are in need.

Financial planning isn't all about money, either. There's more to it. It's about accomplishments, reaching goals, doing what's important to you. It's about your quality of life, however you define it.

Jim Brown quit at the height of his career because he had reached his goals. Now his focus was: "I want to do things for my family. I want to spend time with them. I don't want to be an invalid because I played the game an extra year or two."

Many people feel that way about their careers. The money's nice, they say, but they are doing this for other reasons – to give back to the community or to give back to those who are starting out in the same career, helping them avoid the pitfalls they went through themselves, teaching them the lessons they learned. They mentor other people. The value systems come into play more than just the money.

Jim Brown was ready for a new phase of life; ready to move on to other pursuits, ready to give back. That's what so many of us want. We want to be remembered. We want to be honored for basically being good people. We want to treat our loved ones well, to honor the fans that honored us. We want to go for the extra points.

In football, you can score extra points when you catch the other team in the end zone. They didn't get their ball out on the playing field, and you get a couple of extra points that way. Or you can score a field goal after the touchdown, or get a two-point conversion. You're going for the extras.

In finance, if you consistently do those basic things that will help preserve, protect and grow your assets more efficiently, you can gain those little extra points along the way. In football and in life, they can make all the difference in scoring a win.

You can gain extra points through investments and an estate plan that will hand down your assets as efficiently as possible to the people that you love and care about. You can help them keep more of your money and not give it to the government or attorneys.

The Retirement Account Myth

Let's take a closer look at those retirement plans – those 401(k)s that so many people are counting on and how they really work. People begin them through an empoyer when they are young, understanding that they will fund them with pre-tax dollars – meaning the amount contributed won't face an immediate income tax. The money's going to grow on a tax-advantage basis, which means you don't have to pay any tax on the gains as that account grows. Then you're told that you are going to be in a lower tax bracket in retirement years, so when you do have to pay the deferred tax, you won't have to pay as much.

That third part is a myth for most people because if they have done a good job of accumulating assets, they won't need the money in the retirement account for income. Yet they are required to begin withdrawing it as such and paying income tax on it, whether you want to do so or not. It doesn't make a lot of sense.

Let's say you took $2,000 and put it into an IRA or a 401(k) every year, and you're in a 28 percent tax bracket. You get a $560 tax deduction that year. Let's assume you do that for 30 years and at the end of 30 years, just using the S&P 500 growth rate, you end up with about $427,018 at age 65. So you save about $16,800 in taxes over the course of those years by making the pre-tax contribution, but you end up paying about $119,565 in taxes.

That's assuming taxes stay the same. There's never been a 20-year period of time that taxes haven't gone up in the United States, because about every three years, on average, Congress goes through a major rewrite of the code (www.taxfact.com). Also, remember that the retirement account distribution you'll be required to take will likely force you into a higher tax bracket, affecting your pension and Social Security benefits. There's not many people in retirement who are actually in a lower tax bracket. They're actually in a higher tax bracket, so that third myth that says you're going to be in a lower tax bracket isn't always true. For some people it is, but for the majority of people it's not.

Converting to a Roth IRA

If I had taken that same money and put it into a Roth IRA, which wasn't available 30 years ago, I wouldn't have saved the $560 every year or the $16,800 over the 30 years, but at the end of 30 years I would have $427,018 that's 100 percent tax free.

So does it make sense to save $16,800 in taxes as I go when I end up paying the government over $119,565 in taxes in the future? Or do I go the other way and pay the tax as I go and have a tax-free bucket down the road?

Many people can convert a traditional IRA or 401(k) to a Roth IRA. There are certain rules to follow and we'll run an analysis to see if doing so would be a good move for a client. There are some calculations that we would go through to determine that. For many people, the answer is yes, it does make sense. So the *how you do it* is more of a critical issue.

When you have completed the conversion, you no longer have to take money out of the account if you don't want to, so it's a way to draw a line in the sand and say this is the maximum tax you are going to pay on this account. When money is taken out, the money that you converted and all of the growth on it is tax-free.

In a traditional retirement account, you can figure that you're going to pay the dollar in tax sometime, the question is *when*. You may get a 75 cent discount for paying the tax bill now, but the dollar of liability will come due. If you were the IRS and had a coin machine in which you could put in a quarter and it would spit out a dollar every time, how long would you keep feeding the quarters in – until it ran out of dollars? That's the thought process with these retirement accounts. You're going to pay the tax dollar. So at what point does it make sense to pay it?

The bigger challenge is to come up with the money to pay the tax bill and then be able to let your money grow 100 percent tax free for you and your heirs. It becomes a matter of logistics. There are some financial tools that I call look-alikes that also function with after-tax dollars. The money grows on a tax-advantage basis, and you can get the money out tax free. On those types of tools, the Roth conversion rules do not apply. So there are other ways to get to that same tax-free environment where you no longer have required distributions and you can pass assets down to your heirs without a tax burden.

A Time Bomb for Your Heirs (What Martha Didn't Know)

Otherwise, having this retirement account is a time bomb, and if you don't pay the entire tax bill while you're alive, your heirs will get the honor. That's the situation in which a lot of retirees find themselves. These retirement accounts make up the bulk of their wealth. And at age 70½, they have to start withdrawing the money – and paying the taxes – or else face that 50 percent penalty.

The older you become, the higher the percentage you have to take out. So even if the account stayed the same each year, you would still have to take a little more out each year than the previous. The schedule is set up so that the account will be depleted at an advanced age. You probably don't expect to live to be 116 years old. I don't think anyone who has these accounts really plans to do that, so there's likely going to be money left to heirs – and potentially a substantial amount of money.

Let's say Martha turns 70½ this year and has $500,000 in her IRA. She begins taking out only the required amount, because she doesn't need the money in her situation. If we figure a modest growth rate of six percent and we assume taxes stay the same, when you look at it on a yearly basis, it's not that big of a deal. This year, she had to take out $18,240. At 75, she'll take out $23,928. Each year it increases, and it may force other sources of income into a higher tax bracket.

Over the next 20 years of her life expectancy, she's actually taking out a total of $610,000 from an account that she never needed, and she has to pay a minimum tax of $183,000 on that required distribution. (In this example we're using a 25 percent tax bracket for federal and five for the state. So if both of those are added together, there's a 30 percent tax bracket.) Still, when she's 90, she has $550,000 in this account. She hasn't whittled it down.

Most people would think this account's going to go down to zero, but with a modest growth rate, and with a lower percentage of money required to be taken out, it's very evident in this example that at age 90 she will still have $550,000 that's going to go down to her heirs.

Now at that point in time, the $550,000 is still subject to income tax, but it may also be subject to estate tax both at the federal level and, if there's a state estate tax, at that level as well. When you look at that, an heir could give a large percent of that account back to the federal government, in the form of income and estate taxes.

Martha thought she was going to pass down a large sum of money to her heirs, but she's really only passing down a smaller sum. Uncle Sam, though his tax methodology, is ending up getting a large portion of taxation out of the account during the course of her life and upon her death.

These are the worst tax bombs we can have because people are just not aware. They only look at their tax bill once a year. They think, "Oh well, I've got that account. I've got to take $20,000 out of it this year. I'll pay my tax bill and go on to the next year." But when you look at it over time, it really becomes a huge drain.

How Can You Protect Your Heirs?

There are more efficient ways to get your money into a tax-free environment so you can enhance your quality of life. As we have discussed, you can move it into a Roth, or into a Roth look-alike, and then it will pass tax free to your heirs.

Otherwise, the rules for the heirs at that point say that if Martha did not do any extended planning, the heirs have one of two choices. They pay the tax all at once, or they can spread the taxes over a five-year period, again probably pushing them into a higher tax bracket.

There's a third option with IRA distributions, which is called stretch provisions: If Martha does advance planning and is with the proper vendor, we can actually stretch that tax bill over the course of the heirs' lifetimes. So the tax will probably be the same, but we'll pay a little bit each year. It'll be distributed over thirty to fifty years, depending upon how the account grows and the age of the beneficiary.

In that case the heirs would be required to take out a certain amount every year as well, but it will be at a much, much lower rate because the required minimum distribution for a 25-year-old is a lot less than for a 70-year-old. For example, in the first year that the 25-year-old inherits that account, he may have to take out $1,000. Well on $500,000, do you think it's going to grow greater than $1,000? Sure it is. So that account will continue to grow until that person gets into his mid-50s, early 60s, before the required distribution will be greater than the amount of growth. It wouldn't be unrealistic to see this inherited IRA account distribute a million and a half dollars to the heirs for the same tax liability by implementing stretch provisions.

And what if Martha worries that the children or grandchildren wouldn't be good stewards with their money? By setting up stretch provisions, she can make sure they don't get the money in a lump sum, pay all the tax, and spend the balance on a sports car. If she is concerned the kids won't be good at managing the money, she may be able to use specialized trusts and distribution provisions to require that the heirs can only receive it through an annual distribution on her birthday. So they remember Martha every year when they get that required minimum distribution – and instead of a lump sum, they are guaranteed to have that income stream for the rest of their lives.

Such planning sometimes has to be done in the form of a trust, but it often can be structured solely through the IRA vendor. It depends on the vendor. 401(k) plans don't provide these kind of provisions, and usually with a 401(k) plan the distribution is in a lump sum. No other options. The heirs end up getting hurt a lot if it's a 401(k) that's passing down versus an IRA.

Trouble is, some heirs would prefer the lump sum anyway. They don't see all the hard work that Martha put into amassing that money. They see a Porsche. So when a child is inheriting this kind of money, we really want to talk with Martha ahead of time to make sure she understands the type of person that's going to be receiving this money and how she wants it to be distributed. That's all part of her estate planning process. The conversation goes like this: "Martha, you have this retirement account, there's probably going to be money that's going to be passed down to the heirs. Are they good at managing money? If so, are you concerned if they inherit a large sum of money? If that bothers you, then there are things that we need to do today to make sure that they receive the money in a manner that's best for them based upon your opinion, not their opinion. There are various ways to do that."

If Martha wants to put up some rather complicated restrictions that are beyond the scope of what she might be able to do with a stretch, she'd have to go to an attorney to set up a specialized trust. There are certain planning methodologies that we would give her counsel on. Again, a good retirement quarterback would know what types of strategies those would be and which type of attorneys would be appropriate to consider. Just because an attorney professes to have a lot of experience in retirement planning doesn't mean he or she understands how these trusts can be set up. You really want to explore the background of that attorney and get a specialist. These things are not simple.

Giving to Charities

If Martha decides that she doesn't want to leave anything to the children, or if there are no grandchildren or surviving loved ones to leave the money to, she might choose a charity or a place of worship. We do that the same way as we would if she's giving it to a child. We just name the charity or the organization as the beneficiary with the IRA custodian, then upon her death we file the appropriate paperwork with the IRA custodian and the money is transferred to the charity.

The charity ends up winning, but also the charitable deduction would offset the income tax. Martha's estate would not have to pay income tax on that amount at that point because she's actually giving it to charity.

Therefore if you are planning to do any kind of charitable giving, instead of using after-tax dollars that are subject to capital gains or ordinary income tax, you might use your retirement account money to give that same amount to charities. You can give more by avoiding the taxation.

Wills and Revocable Living Trusts

Among the various types of trusts that can be set up during the course of someone's life is what's known as a revocable living trust. Revocable means you can change it as you go through life. With a will, you have to write a brand new one when you change a beneficiary or any element of your distribution plan. You have to start all over again. With a trust, you can just amend it or change it as you go. A lot of people have gravitated toward the revocable living trust because it accomplishes some things that a will does not.

A will forces all of your assets through the probate system. Everything's public record. You don't have confidentiality. Time is not on your side. The judge and the attorneys determine how soon the accounts can be settled upon your passing. Monies usually will be distributed in a lump sum to each beneficiary. Usually these documents are written on a "honey, I love you" basis – meaning the assets pass first to the surviving spouse, and when the spouse dies they pass equally to the children. Costs of probate can range from three to seven percent of the total assets.

A revocable living trust does several things. It keeps your affairs private and confidential. It'll help eliminate or significantly reduce the probate expenses. And it carries a list of instructions on how you want the money to be distributed.

If a particular heir is not good at managing money, I can set up a payment string so that person can get an income stream for the rest of his or her life. You can put value statements in a trust that offer rewards if the heir takes certain actions. For example, if the recipient goes to college, he may get a little bit more money. If he gets married and has a home, he may have other benefits. Or the recipient may be able to withdraw only the amount of money equal to his W2. So what does this do? It helps to create good stewards of money rather than trust babies who don't work.

A big advantage of a trust over a will is the disability issue. What happens to your affairs if you are no longer able to manage them while you are alive? If you are in a car accident, and recovering in an assisted living facility or nursing home, who has the right to pay your bills and keep your affairs going? A will doesn't come into play at all because you haven't died. With a trust, you have already laid down your list of instructions as to who you want to carry out your wishes and what kind of care you want. You can make sure that your wishes are truly carried out, rather than focusing on financial power of attorney or durable power of attorney. In some states, there's no law that requires a vendor to accept the financial power of attorney. When you have a trust, it eliminates that hassle for disability.

There are other areas where a trust is beneficial. You can put remarriage provisions in them. If a couple has three children, for example, they often want to pledge that the money they worked so hard together to accumulate will eventually go to those children. Otherwise, if the surviving spouse remarries, the new family may be the heirs.

Also with a revocable living trust, if a beneficiary is receiving government assistance of any kind, we can use a special needs provision so the inherited money will be used for the extras and not all of a sudden take away the government assistance. Example: If you inherited $100,000 and were receiving Social Security disability income, you would have to go off SSDI, spend the $100,000 that you inherited, and then go back on the SSDI. With a special needs provision in a revocable living trust, that $100,000 would be set aside and you would still be collecting your Social Security disability. You would reserve that $100,000 for special uses, over and above what your normal assistance would provide.

A trust can accomplish so many more things than a will. It's like packing a suitcase. If you are packing for a vacation, you are going to put a lot of things in that suitcase. You may not use the jacket or the sweater, but it gives you a warm feeling just knowing you have it if you need it. With a trust, you want to make sure that if something occurs, your instructions will be followed. The more detailed you can be, the better it is. A trust enhances your options and makes the distribution much cleaner.

A trust also manages the estate tax issue, if there is any. We try to make sure that we use both parties' exemptions, versus just one as would normally be the case with a will. We wish to take advantage of any federal estate tax exemption or any state estate tax exemption (if applicable). Special provisions can opt out of the estate tax system, letting the money continue to grow for your heirs' benefit. The provisions ensure that your principal and growth never will be subject to estate tax. That can be very, very substantial at the federal level.

We can also protect your wealth from a divorce. It's a possibility that if you die, and a child who inherits your money divorces a few months later, half of the inheritance would go to somebody you disliked and never intended as a beneficiary. You can expect that person will scoop up the money and say, "See ya."

It's pathetic to think all of your hard work in accumulating those dollars may have contributed to the breakup of a marriage because of the greed it caused in the human heart. Things like that happen. There are steps you can take to make sure your money goes to the people you love and care for.

You can also add protection against creditors and judgments. Let's say you pull out in front of a bus and the crash kills four people. You exhaust all your limits of liability on your auto policy, you exhaust your umbrella limit, and you still have a half million dollar judgment against you. If you have just inherited a half million dollars from Martha, that money's subject to that creditor and can be taken away. However, a trust can include provisions to make sure a creditor cannot get to that $500,000 of inherited money.

Even with all of the advantages of doing some distribution planning with wills or trusts, you still find people who have done nothing, and the consequences can be grievous. This is an area where we find most people procrastinate. They know they need to get around to it but never do, or they did it way back when their kids were little to set up a guardianship. And nothing has been changed since.

If you die with a will, that's fine – but your estate goes through the probate court and is subject to the costs of probate. You may have estate tax costs as well. In turn, far less money goes to the heirs. That wasn't what you intended, but because you didn't get around to it, or didn't know that those fees would be levied and certain entities would get paid before the heirs, you have allowed your money to be legally stolen from you.

Dealing With What's Difficult

You can almost understand the procrastination. It's hard to deal with these issues. It's hard to confront face-to-face the fact that you're mortal. You think you are going to live forever, but in a twinkle, life may be taken away, or you may be disabled. There are a lot of forces we don't control, and putting instructions down on paper says a lot about how much we really love those we're leaving behind.

A good retirement quarterback is going to take a person through that process because it isn't complicated. It's just a matter of saying let's get your current wishes down on paper and maybe look three to five years out. Don't look twenty or thirty years in the future, because you're going to change it anyway. Life throws things at us that we do not anticipate. You are going to have a different set of beneficiaries possibly with grandchildren and great grandchildren and so forth. You may have different causes and charities that you want to support. Those things will ebb and flow.

Ask yourself this: "If I were to die today, how would I like my assets to be distributed?" That gives you a frame of reference, a starting point. Then you can move forward and focus on efficiency and getting the money to the people you love and care about. You will be going for those extra points.

For a typical couple, one spouse will be responsible for certain tasks, while the other will have different talents and responsibilities. So as an example, the wife may be raising the kids and making the decisions on schooling and paying the regular bills, but the husband usually has done the big-picture stuff and he's been taking care of investing the long-term growth money. Often that marriage has worked very, very well. Each spouse has an opinion, but each makes the decisions in his or her areas of strength.

What happens if that person is disabled or is no longer here? Perhaps a wife who has never paid a bill in her life is suddenly responsible for assuring she can continue her lifestyle. The husband took care of all the big financial decisions. She really needs a good quarterback on her side making sure her income is guaranteed, her lifestyle is guaranteed, she's not paying too much in taxes, and so forth.

Your wealth adviser can also help you set up a continuity plan – that is, an assurance of consistency in the advice you're getting now from your advisor and lawyers and the advice that your spouse and your heirs will get if you're gone. You want to make sure future generations know the game plan, and they remain good stewards of that money. You worked too hard for anything less.

CHAPTER 6

DON'T GET SACKED!

Defensive Maneuvers to Protect Your Hard Work

Imagine you're the quarterback. The ball is in your hand. You're surveying the field. Who's where, what's developing? It's decision time. A lot of weight is bearing down on you. What if your play doesn't go as expected? Will your offensive line be there for you?

When you need protection, you need insurance. We all have exposures to potential loss. Whether driving your car or just getting older, you face financial exposure. What is the potential for loss? Are you going to self-fund it and just take assets that you have worked hard to amass and pay for whatever might arise, or do you purchase insurance in which a third party comes in and takes care of those losses?

You may decide to self-fund the smaller liabilities, but for the larger ones – let's say you are at fault in a deadly five-car pileup – you want to make sure you have a lot of liability protection so your assets aren't on the line. You have worked too hard to accumulate them to have them swept away.

We'll look at those assets and consider the different levels of insurance. We'll look at the auto insurance and make sure you're not paying for coverage you don't need and your limits of liability are adequate based upon your assets. We'll look at the homeowner's policy, the umbrella policy, and any floaters you may have. We'll look at your health insurance: A lot of retirees are on Medicare or a Medicare supplement form, and we'll want to make sure all of those coverages are adequate.

A lot of people have misconceptions about Medicare and what it does and doesn't cover. Some people think Medicare will provide long-term-care protection, and it doesn't. Medicare will pay for reha-bilitative care as long as your health is improving. But even that benefit is for a limited time. Once it stops, you may continue to incur expenses but end up paying for them out of your assets. If you are in the facility for an extended period, all your life savings could be drained. It's not unusual to have $50,000 or $75,000 of expenses every year at such a facility. It doesn't take long to spend down assets.

Most people whom we work with have enough assets that it would make no sense to try to spend down their money in advance so the federal government, through Medicaid, would pay for all their care, including long-term.

A couple must consider if they start spending money for the care of one, what effect will that have on the survivor? What lifestyle will the surviving spouse be able to maintain? It's a critical scenario that must be addressed. It's not so much a question of whether we will reach the stage where we may need long-term care. The question, increas-ingly, is when. Statistically, one in two will be in a nursing home for about an average of two-and-a-half years sometime between age 65 and death *(Source: Genworth 2012 Cost of Care Survey, conducted by CareScout®, April 2012)*. At what point will you need help?

Will a health issue arise to keep you from your daily chores so you need to pay people to do them for you? Or will you just be slowed by normal aging? In either case, 97 percent of people in that age group will use some of their assets for care – whether for heavy chores, or the cooking and cleaning, or whatever the need may be *(source: Genworth 2012 Cost of Care Survey, conducted by CareScout®, April 2012)*.

Long-term care is one area a lot of people try to self-fund. It's probably not the wisest decision because they will spend down a significant amount of assets very quickly. But long-term-care planning is like drafting a will: Most people have thought about it but think it is too expensive and don't know alternative ways to get that same benefit without the cost.

Many people consider a traditional long-term-care policy, which provides a daily benefit or monthly benefit to cover custodial or in-home care. Just like your home or auto coverage, you pay a premium, and if you do not use the policy for benefits, you lose the premiums.

Or they may look at an asset-based approach to long-term care. If you have an asset you are not using for living expense, per se, and can set aside for an emergency, you can actually leverage that to create long-term-care benefits without incurring any expense. That option has been around for 15 years or so, but we find most people have never been exposed to the asset-based approach.

There are other long-term-care benefits, such as Aid and Attendance for Veterans. It's one of those little-known benefits that veterans have. If they served during wartime and their assets fall within a certain range, they can get a long-term-care benefit for themselves and their spouses. Sometimes we can find free coverage or funding for which they qualify.

Life insurance is another way to make sure assets transfer efficiently from one generation to the next. If you want to guarantee your heirs will receive a certain amount of money, the least expensive way to do that is to buy a life insurance contract, which takes pennies to create dollars. The sooner you die, the higher the return on investment. From a financial standpoint it's a leverage tool. You are leveraging dollars today to create many more dollars down the road which somebody will receive, usually income-tax free. Newer versions of life insurance can also provide long-term-care benefits, should you need them.

Insurance isn't always the answer, though often it may be the least expensive option. For asset protection, we need to examine your potential exposures and make sure all circumstances are considered. That's all part of the insurance review. Life insurance at the federal level can be subject to estate taxes, and we find most people are not aware of that. If you have life insurance in play and you don't need it, there are ways to get out of that coverage efficiently.

You should turn over every stone with your wealth adviser, looking at the consequences and at the potential advantages and disadvantages. If you do that in plenty of time, you can still have a good nest egg to pass on to your heirs.

New Approaches to Long-Term-Care Protection

Retirees often presume that if you don't arrange for long-term care a generation before you die or before you need it, then it's going to be prohibitively expensive. But there are financial tools that allow you to have this benefit without great expense – or any at all – and without any medical review. You don't have to qualify for the benefit; it will be there if you need it. It makes a lot of sense to consider those financial tools, but you need to work with someone who knows where they are in the marketplace and how to apply them.

As an example, there are some hybrid annuities in the marketplace now that you may use to create an income stream you cannot outlive. Let's say you're getting your $10,000 a year guaranteed for the rest of your life. If three years into the annuity, you find yourself in a long-term-care facility, the provisions of some of those tools will double the income and they'll give you $10,000 of additional income while that condition lasts or for a specified time period. So you're getting $10,000 of income from your financial tool and getting another $10,000 from the insurance company because you qualify for the long-term-care benefit. It's a way to get some additional benefits without incurring any additional expense – and without having to go through medical underwriting to see if you qualify.

Health issues weigh heavily on the minds of many retirees. They worry not only about their physical health but whether their medical needs will ravage their financial health. Such fears can easily be averted. With professional help, you can weigh your options and secure your future. A good quarterback can help you make the successful plays.

WINNING THE GAME

Remember when you were a teenager and knew it all? "You'll see someday," your mom or dad said. Then later you realized you were becoming your parents. It's the nature of wisdom: As you mature, you become more willing to tap into the knowledge of others.

By the time you reach retirement age, you likely have learned the hard lessons in life. If you haven't lived through the ups and downs of the financial markets – and many baby boomers did indeed come to believe the markets would trend ever upward – you might not be able to see what might happen to you.

That's when a good wealth adviser is crucial: By delegating financial dealings to someone who has seen it all, you gain reassurance. A good wealth advisor has seen variations of your story many, many times.

Any worthy CEO knows how to delegate responsibility. He or she doesn't know it all alone and therefore has assistants and advisers with specialties. That's all part of good leadership. In retirement, you, too, should delegate – to accountants, attorneys, your wealth adviser, all of your choosing. You don't lose control. You gain a corporate knowledge. You might think of yourself as the CEO of your portfolio.

Although this book has primarily contained advice for retirees, younger readers would do well to heed these words. Some of these strategies require action long before retirement. At any age, you want to have some investment strategies that give you safer, secure growth. The earlier you learn some of these fundamentals, the more successful you're going to be when you finally get into retirement.

If we can teach our clients' children some of those fundamentals, we can get them to be better players before they reach retirement. When they get to the point where they have a family and are taking on debt, that's when some of these principles come into play.

That's why we routinely hold family meetings. We bring the children in for discussions because they may or may not have talked to mom and dad about what happens *if* – as in what they would do if their parents became ill. "Here's the planning that we have done for your parents," we tell them, "and here's why we have done it, and here's how it benefits you. Here's who you call if something happens." When the kids come out of meetings like that, it's as if a burden has been lifted off their shoulders – particularly if their parents are older and are starting to show signs of mental or physical incapacity.

Today in this "sandwich" society, some couples not only have children they must take care of, but they also are helping in some way to take care of their parents. That calls for carefully devised strategies, and getting that playbook established for such a couple makes the situation easier for the entire family.

Here's what I would say to a young person just starting out: Pay yourself first, and be very cautious about whether a purchase is something you need or merely a want. Many people, and the young in particular, take on excessive debt without a guaranteed way to pay. Then when life takes that job away, or they have a disability, they are in a financial pinch.

Young people need to learn such fundamentals as putting some of the pay raise aside for their retirement program. The earlier they start the better. It's amazing the difference that even one year will have thirty years in the future. That's what compounding does. Many of my clients are retirees who are fairly well off – and that's because they did sound planning early in life. Perhaps someone shared words of wisdom with them to set them on the right track. But without that planning, they wouldn't have the assets today to worry about.

Whether or not you have been very successful, the question at retirement age is this: Are you doing the things from this point forward that will minimize your exposures? No matter your age, and no matter how big your bucket of money, you really need professional advice.

If you had a time machine and could go back five years with the knowledge you have today, would you make any changes in dealing with your finances? Most people would acknowledge they certainly would. I only hope if I were to ask you that same question five years from now, you would shrug and say, "No, I am confident I have been doing the best I could." My hope is you begin those changes now to deal proactively instead of reactively to get your finances in better shape.

You've made your drive into the end zone for the final touchdown. Yes, it took wits and power to get you here, but it also took perseverance, patience and faith in the playbook. You've trusted in the talents and protection of your teammates. And you have come to appreciate the savvy of your quarterback in helping to put the big game plan into action. Knowing he's got your back has helped you make the right decisions.

Thorough planning for your retirement is an investment in your peace of mind. You can know you can do the things you want to do during life. You can be confident that you can continue the lifestyle you have grown accustomed to without running out of money, even in your final years if you should need constant care. You can know you can pass that money on to the people you love and care about, as efficiently as possible with the least amount of expense. That's when you know you have focused – you have done your planning properly.

I've met so many retirees who are doing all right but are afraid of what they don't know. They face so many unknowns because they are not working with trained professionals. They're trying to make their own way as best they can. The majority of people are doing a lot of things well. But because they don't know some of the rules or the tools or the laws, they are not planning efficiently. They're paying too much in taxes and subjecting their heirs to expenses and complications that could be avoided.

A good financial quarterback will help finesse the plays so you can focus on the quality-of-life issues, whatever that means to you. Family, friends, and the things you believe in – that's really what life's about. That's why you worked so hard. What you want is to move forward boldly into retirement, pursuing your dreams, confident that you have done right for yourself and the generations ahead.

And that's what I want for you.

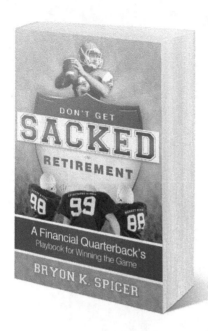

How can you use this book?

Why have a custom version of *Don't Get Sacked In Retirement?*

- Build personal bonds with customers, prospects, employees, donors, and key constituencies
- Develop a long-lasting reminder of your event, milestone, or celebration
- Provide a keepsake that inspires change in behavior and change in lives
- Deliver the ultimate "thank you" gift that remains on coffee tables and bookshelves
- Generate the "wow" factor

Books are thoughtful gifts that provide a genuine sentiment that other promotional items cannot express. They promote employee discussions and interaction, reinforce an event's meaning or location, and they make a lasting impression. Use your book to say "Thank You" and show people that you care.